EDUCATION FOR PEACE

Dr. USHA RAO

M.A. (Phil.), M.A. (Psy.), M.Ed., Ph.D.
Former Principal of Gokhale Education Society's
College of Education & Research,
Parel, Mumbai - 400 012.

Himalaya Publishing House
ISO 9001 : 2015 CERTIFIED

First Edition : 2012
Reprint : 2016
Reprint : 2024

Published by	:	Mrs. Meena Pandey for **HIMALAYA PUBLISHING HOUSE PVT. LTD.,** "Ramdoot", Dr. Bhalerao Marg, Girgaon, Mumbai - 400 004. **Phone:** 022-23860170, 23863863; **Fax:** 022-23877178 **E-mail:** himpub@bharatmail.co.in; **Website:** www.himpub.com
Branch Offices	:	
New Delhi	:	"Pooja Apartments", 4-B, Murari Lal Street, Ansari Road, Darya Ganj, New Delhi - 110 002. Phone: 011-23270392, 23278631; Fax: 011-23256286
Nagpur	:	Kundanlal Chandak Industrial Estate, Ghat Road, Nagpur - 440 018. Phone: 0712-2738731, 2721216
Bengaluru	:	Plot No. 91-33, 2nd Main Road Seshadripuram, Behind Nataraja Theatre, Bengaluru-560020. Phone: 08041138821, 9379847017, 9379847005
Hyderabad	:	No. 3-4-184, Lingampally, Besides Raghavendra Swamy Matham, Kachiguda, Hyderabad - 500 027. Phone: 040-27560041, 27550139
Chennai	:	No. 34/44, Motilal Street, T. Nagar, Chennai - 600 017. Mobile: 09380460419
Pune	:	First Floor, "Laksha" Apartment, No. 527, Mehunpura, Shaniwarpeth (Near Prabhat Theatre), Pune - 411 030. Phone: 020-24496323/24496333; Mobile: 09370579333
Cuttack	:	Plot No 5F-755/4, Sector-9, CDA Market Nagar, Cuttack - 753 014, Odisha. Mobile: 09338746007
Kolkata	:	3, S.M. Bose Road, Near Gate No. 5, Agarpara Railway Station, North 24 Parganas, West Bengal - 700109. Mobile: 09674536325
DTP by	:	Sudhakar Shetty (HPH Pvt. Ltd., Mumbai)
Printed at	:	Trinity Academy, Mumbai. On behalf of HPH.

PREFACE

It is a well-known fact that most of our citizens are not familiar with the constitution and their innocence is dragged by unscrupulous people to gain their ends. In this respect, it is essential that our people should steadily increase their awareness about this aspect; and this book has attempted to fulfil the felt need. It has been written in a very simple way to enable the students to understand the matter.

In fact, concern for 'Peace-Education' has been widely expressed by various commissions, great industrialists, good sportsmen and above all by many principals of the schools as well as colleges. This aspect was taken (felt) by me as a great challenge and my attention was focussed on learning students both in schools and in colleges.

In addition, almost every day the newspapers too are increasingly talking about issues like rape, political conflict, murders, thefts, etc. which went on pouring in my mind that I must start writing on the subject of 'Peace' and 'Peace Education'

This book attempts to outline, the content of 'Education For Peace'. In fact, the subject of Peace-Education is not a separate subject; but a perspective from which all subjects are to be taught. The book is useful to the teachers, teachers-educators, politicians, peace-reporters, peace-activists, peace-research students and also to those who wish to write volumes of papers on Peace-Education. Besides the above said facts, Shri Kaustubhji from Himalaya Publishing House Pvt. Ltd. also was telling me again and again on writing a book on 'Peace Education'! This he did deliberately because there was an inclusion of the subject on Peace Education in the B.Ed. Syllabus. All the thing put together, I thought of writing on peace-education; and I then knew that this really gave me an opportunity to improve my writing capacity while presenting the ideas! Result is the current tiny book in your hand!

I am really grateful to all those teachers and teacher educators who willingly helped me in my task. So too, I am thankful to Shri Kaustubhji who inspired me to write.

It is sincerely felt that many school administrators, teachers, as well as teacher-educators who read this book will be motivated to be able to contribute to World-Peace. A committed teacher is always creative and innovative with and in his or her professional work chosen. In this connection, it can be truely said that it is the individual drop that makes the ocean.

Last but not the least, I am indebted to Lord Shri Krishna, who gave me lot of strength mental as well as physical to complete the work undertaken. Millions of thanks to HIM!

USHA RAO

JAI SRI KRISHNA

CONTENTS

1. Defining Peace 1

2. Analysis of Indian Society 40

3. Conflict Analysis 59

4. Bringing about Change By Peaceful Means 77

5. Towards A Culture of Peace 114

6. Agencies In Peace-keeping And Peace-building 130

Bibliography 161

ATTAINMENT OF WORLD PEACE THROUGH PRACTICE OF BUDDHISM

1

DEFINING PEACE

INTRODUCTION

It is only when we start examining the lives of great people that we come across, the question of peace enters in! So is the case of education. Deeper examination of education demands that it should be peace-oriented. And, peace-oriented education becomes possible only when one gets a clear picture of peace-oriented life! The term 'peace' is always taken as substitute for calmness and compassion. On this meaning of the term, there is no unanimity. It is, of course, interpreted in different ways. Peace is something that is considered good such as love, kindness, honesty, contentment and simplicity. Education today, is no more considered in isolation as a discipline, but it has to be considered in the context of social and national values. In fact, education iso transmission of life by the living, through the living and for the living. It is just because of the degradation of spiritual values. That, today the pupils are getting addicted to TV, computer, night-parties, clubs, etc., is a fact which no one will deny. Advancement of comforts in life has reduced the conscience of a person. If this is the case, then pupil's moral and ethical development will be definitely at a decrease. Where will 'PEACE' enter in such a situation?

Let us now get into ourselves in the following story which reads thus —

Meera, a very good looking woman, round about thirty years in age was waiting on a busy bus stop. She was a mentally restarted woman and Vijay was fully knowing about this fat in details. As Meera was waiting for a particular bus to take her to work, Vijay stopped his car and offered her a lift telling Meera that he is also going right to the place where she is working. Without any hesitation, Meera very willingly stepped into the car and sat very comfortably by the side of Vijay. But Meera was taken by Vijay to a secluded spot, raped her and brought her back to the usual bus stop! Vijay had actually compelled Meera for sexual contact by coaxing and threatening her. A case of sexual abuse indeed. Vijay never cared to think of any sort of consequences of this act, whether, whatever that happened was good or bad, correct or wrong. In fact, such instances are constantly witnessed by the society and each one of us is witnessing this with a bitter taste. In fact, there are many such instances. Hence, there is a global need for developing a new religion that preaches a philosophy of social organisation, and universal brotherhood. There is great need to develop ethical values, and, there is also a universal need to create such ethical values that are based on love, devotion, mercy and sacrifice. But what is seen today is a nuclear competition that has led to the destruction of mankind. When looked from the materialistic point of view, there is no denying the fact that, today's society has achieved a lot to fulfill the materialistic needs. Man, thus, has everything except a peace of mind! One can clearly observe the erosion of values in the day-to-day life. Instances of increasing crime and violence at different places are enough to make one understand that today's society is experiencing a peace-crisis. Today's society is experiencing a peace-crisis. Today's modern educational system has hardly any time to concentrate on the spiritual development of the child. Because of lack of correct awareness, there is failure on the part of our children to exercise their own inner minds. More emphasis is put today on gaining good marks in the examination, securing well-salaried jobs, and so on. What is needed most today is the establishment of spiritual centres, where spiritual values will be taught to shape the human behaviour. If a person is not able to distinguish between correct and wrong, good or bad, how can a good conduct be expected from him or her? It is only through the teaching of ethical values, a person will be able to distinguish between good and bad, between correct and wrong. Our thoughts, our intellect and our emotions are the products of our mind; therefore, great emphasis should be put on the betterment of mind, wherein, there will be inculcation of ethical and moral values. But alas! Today, running after immediate pleasure, has become more important than spiritual development; and today's education is very busy in the development of the intellect of the child whose mind, soul, thoughts are kept unnourished! Scientific and technical study may increase pupil's knowledge and sharpen his or her memory; but, without learning to apply the power of reasoning to the subjects like literature, social sciences, history, philosophy, etc.; pupils are not adequately prepared for the breadth and depth of human life. Today's fast life has madness for money and this has been mistaken for 'good progress'. He or she is physically exhausted and mentally depressed! Technology has gone hand in hand with criminals. There is high-tech forgery and high-tech serial killing. For politicians, lie has become a key-weapon for their survival. Hence, for all such quoted aspects 'peace-education' is the only solution.

Because of the above discussion, it is to be stated here that the entire education system [along with curriculum activities] must aim at inculcating ethical consciousness, and it is we, the teachers should make a beginning from our inner hearts. For the global happiness and true prosperity of mankind, peace-education is a must — PEACE EDUCATION IS A MUST ...!

However, the question now jumps like a boomrang — 'What is this Peace-Education?' — 'What is the meaning of the term 'peace'? etc. etc. Hence, it is now essential to understand the making of the term 'peace' and also to know about the concept of 'peace-education.'

❖ Peace: Its Definition

Several years ago Leo Sandy entered into a dialogue with fellow veterans to explore the definition of peace, and based on their own experiences of war to provide a satisfactory account that could serve as a guide for all peace-makers who seek a world without war.

'Peace' is a word that is uttered almost as frequently as "truth", "beauty" and "love". It may be just as elusive to define as these other virtues. Common synonyms for 'peace' include "amity", "friendship", "harmony", "concord" "tranquility", "response", "truce", "pacification" and "neutrality." While certain of these descriptions are appropriate, they are still quite limited in describing nature of peace.

In its most limited type of definition, peace is the mere absence of war.

Reardon [1988] insists that 'peace is the absence of violence in all is forms — physical, social, psychological and structural. But, this, as a definition, is unduly negative in that it fails to provide any affirmative picture of peace or its ingredients [Copi and Cohen, p. 195].

In its most myopic and limited definition, 'Peace is the mere absence of war.' O'Kane (1992) sees this definition as a "vacuous, passive, simplistic, and unresponsive escape mechanism too often resorted to in the past — without success". This definition also commits a serious oversight: it ignores the residual feelings of mistrust and suspicion that the winners and losers of war harbor toward each other. The subsequent suppression of mutual hostile feelings is not taken into account by those who define peace so simply. Their stance is that as long as people are not actively engaged in overt, mutual, violent, physical and destructive activity, then peace exists. This, of course, is another way of defining cold 'peace' to states of affairs that are not truly peaceful (Copi and Cohen, p. 194). Unfortunately, this definition of peace appears to be prevailing in the world.

A peace which depends upon the threat and intention to kill vast number of human beings is hardly a justifiable peace worthy of the name.

Word 'PEACE' is more effective and meaningful when it is adopted according to the social and cultural context and the needs of a country. It should be enriched by its cultural and spiritual values together with the universal human values. It should also be globally relevant. Peace could be defined in many ways. There is no universally accepted definition as such 'Peace' is holistic. It embraces the physical, emotional, intellectual and social growth within a framework deeply rooted in traditional human values. It is based on philosophy that teachers love, compassion, trust, fairness, cooperation and reverence for the human family and all life on our beautiful planet.

Peace is like a skill-building. It empowers children to use creative and non-destructive ways to settle conflict and to live in harmony with themselves, others and their world... Peace-building is the task of every human being and the challenge of the human family.

The basic concept embedded in the above definitions are that peace is a remedial measure to protect children from falling into the ways of violence in society. It aims at the total development of the child, and also tries to inculcate higher human and social values in the mind of the child. In essence, it attempts to develop a set of behavioural skills necessary for peaceful living. In fact, two out of the four pillars of education as stated by Dolor Report, namely learning to live together and learning to be, are related to peaceful living. What matters most is the integration of peaceful attitudes.

Peace is possible for life at all stages and it is upto man to choose his destiny or to suffer from the horrors of war. Today, mankind is at the cross-road where he has to choose with courage, determination and imagination.

Peace is possible for life at all stages. At this moment in our history, peace is only a dream that is far from the actual daily reality of the majority of the world population and the rest of God's creation on earth. India is a multi-cultural, multi-ethnic and multi-religious nation and has to learn to live with it to its best advantage. In the language of UNESCO, 'War begins in the minds of men.' Hence, the remedy also has to take shape in the human minds; and so, there is a great need to train human minds to work towards peace.

Peace is being quiet in within. It is having a good feeling inside. Peace is when people get along and do not argue or hit. Peace is having positive thoughts about others and myself. Peace is more than the absence of war. Peace is living in harmony and not fighting with others.

Peace is a relaxed state of mind. Peace consists of pure feeling and good wishes. World-peace goes through nonviolence, acceptance, fairness and communication. Peace is the main characteristic of a civilized society.

Peace on earth begins in the heart and mind of each individual. The sum of the attitudes projected by every citizen influences the well-being of one's family, community and the future of life on earth. It has been very rightly said by Mahatma Gandhi thus —

> *"If we are to reach real peace in the world, we shall have to begin with children. And, if they will group up in their natural innocence, we do net have to pass fruitless ideal resolutions, but we shall go from love to love and peace to peace, until at last all the corners of the world we covered with peace and love for which consciously or unconsciously the whole world is hungering."*

So too, rightly said by A.J. Muste — "There is no way to peace. Peace is the way." Accordingly to readings of Bible — "The peace makers shall be called the children of God."

Such definitions are useful in their own fields of work. But when they are taken as the only peace then there is the tendency to ignore the other perspectives. All the perspectives of peace contain the seed of peace.

The word peace is mostly used in a narrow sense to mean absence of war. Surely it is more than that. It should mean not only absence of war, but violence in all forms such as conflict, threat to life, social degradation, discrimination, oppression, exploitation, poverty, injustice and so on. Peace cannot be built as long as violent social structures exist in society. Naturally such structures will lead people to act violently. For instance, an unfair system of resource distribution in a society leads to frustration of those who get less. Frustration leads people to violence. Absence of all such obstructive and in conducive factors to a good life can be called negative peace.

All the above perspectives imply that peace is an external phenomenon There is a perspective quite different to it, which holds that peace is an inner factor. It says 'Peace is within you.'

All ranges of shades of meanings of peace come easily under three basic sources. They are inner peace, social peace and peace with nature. They could be analyzed further this way:

(1) Inner Peace;

(2) Social Peace: For example, harmony and peace with oneself, good health, and absence of inner conflicts, joy, sense of freedom, insight, spiritual peace, and feelings of kindness, compassion, and content, appreciation of art.

For example, peace between man and man, (men and women as well) harmony arising from human relationships at all levels, conflict reconciliation and resolution, love, friendship, unity, mutual understanding, acceptance, co-operation, brotherhood, tolerance of differences, democracy, community-building, human rights, morality.

(3) Peace with Nature: For example, harmony with natural environment and mother earth.

❖ Basic Concept of Peace

Peace in more than the absence of violence. It is basically a process constructed through research, training and practice. It focuses mainly on human behaviour attitudes and responses to a changing environment. Peace is social value. It eradicates prejudices and differences. It promotes equality and social justice. Peace is a positive sign in history bringing people together, eliminating suspicion and mistrust. Put into simpler language when we talk of peace we expect at least three basic conditions: communication, cooperation, confidence. The ideal is to have the three of them working at the same time. UNESCO'S constitution highlights these as prerequisite in the preamble "ignorance of each others ways and lives has been a common cause, throughout the history mankind, of that suspicion and mistrust between the peoples of the world through which their differences have all too often broken into war." Ignorance is a result of lack of communication: suspicion and mistrust show that confidence building has not taken place; the fact that differences break into armed conflicts indicates that cooperative techniques have failed to give tangible results. Can the future of peace-education be based upon these fundamental principles?

In spite of whatever has been discussed so far, we need to understand the concept of peace in more details. While students have a concrete concept of war, their concept of peace is often abstrait. Before we go in for further discussion, the following questions will help to clarify our concept of peace as concrete as well as positive and life affirming.

- Is peace only the absence of war?
- Is Mumbai city with its high rate of robbery, murder, rape, at peace?
- Is peace only the absence of violence?
- Is peace the absence of physical and psychological violence?
- Is it the hallmark of just and caring society?
- What kind of peace is it if people in villages do not have safe water to drink and medicines to heal, when they are ill and dying, when babies die in thousands for want of food and nutrition and footpaths are their beds at night?
- Is it possible sometimes to use violence in order to achieve social justice and thus assure a more enduring lasting peace?
- Is peace concerned with the destruction of our planet by pollution, inordinate needs and also indiscriminate use of our resources?
- Is peace only created because of the world outside or do we have to look at the world within and our own individual as well as our school value systems?

Pondering over the above questions will lead us to an understanding of the deeper meaning of peace.

The live basic values that most religions teach are derived from the domain of our personality.

— Right conduct – Physical domain
— Truth – Intellectual domain
— Love – Psychic domain
— Non-violence – Spiritual domain
— Peace – Emotional domain

Peace thus embodies the essence of the four values mentioned above and only a harmonious development of the spiritual, psychic, intellectual and physical domains of man's personality will result in the "peace" of the whole person.

The human soul is a spark of divinity. The same spark can be found in each and every human being when the externals are stripped way. With this realisation is the truth revealed to us. Righteous conduct refers not only to our code of conduct with respect to self, but includes conduct for the well-being of all. Love is the energy that transmits and transforms all forms of life. It is the greatest force on earth. True love comes from the attributes of peace: compassion, selflessness and forgiveness. When there is universal love, self no longer thinks of 'oneself' but the 'other self.' Extension of love is nonviolence. Nonviolence is at the heart of peacemaking. It is also the work of reconciling enemies, promoting justice and ending war.

Peace is the culmination of above values. It is the fulcrum of existence. Nothing in the universe can have as profound an effect on our lives as the absence of peace within us. When we are emotionally disturbed and not at peace with ourselves or others, there is restlessness and confusion. We do not see the world and its affairs or even our own actions in the right perspective.

"Peace follows enlightenment, when man establishes peace at heart, no external force can disturb it."

— Bhagwan Buddha

After having discussed so much about **Peace** and its **Nature**, let us now think about the types of peace.

TYPES OF PEACE

We all have need which can be best understood by Maslow's hierarchy of learning. If the needs are not satisfied, then the person is not in the pleasurable state. Therefore, there is always the ways to satisfy the needs and the individual uses all his or her power to satisfy them. In the process of gratifying their need, individual sometimes resort to the measures where they hamper the peace within themselves and outside.

Peace is an idealistic term and rarely there will be suitable peace, which means that peace can be achieved but maintaining it is very difficult.

Peace also does not mean the total absence of any conflicts. It means the absence of violence in any form and resolving the conflict in a constructive way. There is a distinction sometimes made between 'Negative Peace' and 'Positive Peace.' [*Galtung*, 1996].

Peace as the mere absence of war is what Woolman (1985) refers to as "Negative Peace." This definition is based on Johan Galtung's ideas of peace. For Galtung, negative peace is defined as a state acquiring a set of social structures that provide security and protection from acts of direct physical violence committed by individuals, groups or nations. The emphasis is on control of violence. The main strategy is dissociation, whereby conflicting parties are separated. In general, policies based on the idea of negative peace do not deal with the causes of violence, only its manifestations. Therefore, these policies are thought to be really insufficient to assure lasting conditions of peace. Indeed, by suppressing the release of tensions resulting from social conflict, negative peace efforts may actually lead to future violence of greater magnitude (*Woolman*, 1985).

The recent wars in the former Yugoslovia are testimony to this. The massive military machine previously provided by the U.S.S.R. put a lid on ethnic hostilities yet did nothing to resolve them thus allowing them to fester and erupt later.

Positive peace, in contrast, is "a pattern of cooperation and integration between major human groups .... [It] is about people interacting in cooperative ways; it is about social organizations of diverse peoples who willingly choose to cooperate for the benefit of all humankind; it calls for a system in which there are no winners and losers — all are winners; it is a state so highly valued that institutions are built around it to protect and promote it" (O'Kane, 1991-92). It also "involves the search for positive conditions which can resolve the underlying causes of conflict that produce violence" (Woolman, 1985, p. 8). The strategies used for this purpose are called "associative," and they are characterized by "a high level of social interaction [which] enables morc rapid resolution of conflict by providing maximum contacts through which solutions may arise"

(Woolman, 1985, p. 8). Woolman also describes the sort of social reorganization that would provide the best opportunity for real peace. Essentially, he espouses Galtung's idea of smallness and decentralization of power and authority. Thus, "small scale social organization offers a better environment for encouragement of local autonomy, participation, and high levels of inter-group interaction. Big countries, corporations, and institutions are generally regarded as negative structures because they are prone to depersonalization, excessive centralization of decision-making, and patterns of center-periphery exploitation." Gene Sharp (1980) in his Social Power and Political Freedom adroitly elaborates these points. The condition of smallness does much to reduce feelings of anonymity and powerlessness. It also facilitates the development of relationships which can restore and preserve community values and spiritual needs which "should take precedence over the materialism that is so central to Western culture." (*Woolman*, 1985, p. 12).

Consistent with these approaches, Reardon (1988) places global justice as the central concept of positive peace and asserts that "justice, in the sense of the full enjoyment of the entire range of human rights by all people, is what constitutes positive peace" (p.26).

In a similar vain, Trostle's (1992) comprehensive definition of peace clearly places it within a positive context.

[Peace is] a state of well-being that is characterized by trust, compassion, and justice. In this state, we can be encouraged to explore as well as celebrate our diversity, and search for the good in each other without the concern for personal pain and sacrifice... It provides us a chance to look at ourselves and others as part of the human family, part of one world.

It is difficult not to see in these "positive" approaches to the definition of "peace" radical implications for a reorganization of our society and, indeed, our entire world. There is no denying that a positive conception of peace along the lines suggested by Galtung, Sharp, Reardon, et al. would involve fundamental changes on the level of the individual psyche and the nation-state as well. At both levels, genuine peace requires the advent of a new selflessness, a willingness to see our fellow humans as our brothers and sisters, and — as the traditional religions have always conciled — to love them as we love ourselves.

But besides this subjective component of each individual's altruistic love, there must be justice which depends on the right sort of social organization. This is Reardon's point. It is also implied by Trostle's "state of well-being... of global harmony... part of one world." The suggestion here is that, at the very least, a state of (genuine) peace is something beyond what can be achieved by the traditional system of sovereign nation-states. The problem, of course, is that this system lacks a system of workable law, each state being the ultimate arbiter of whether it will wield force in its pursuit of national interest or not. Without workable world law it's hard to see how there can be justice, and so, peace, in its true sense. The world federalists have expressed this point succinctly but powerfully: "There can be no world peace without international justice; no international justice without world law; and no effective world law without institutions to make, interpret and enforce it." And the world federalists may be right when they make this requirement of enforceable world law a sine qua non for the abolition of the age-old institution of war itself. Certainly Albert Einstein thought so when he declared that "Peace is not merely the absence of war but the presence of justice, of law, of order — in short, of government" (*Einstein*, 1968).

In conclusion, we believe that a proper definition of "peace" must include positive characteristics over and above the mere absence of belligerence. Rather, it must include those positive factors that foster cooperation among human groups with ostensibly different cultural patterns so that social justice can be done and human potential can freely develop within democratic political structures. And this — promoting social justice/freedom by democratic means — will almost certainly require more "selfless" concern at all levels: at the personal level, more brotherly love; and at the international level, less narrow national self-interest — a goal which we believe will require a diminution of the current system of nation states and the gradual emergence of a world community self-governed by world law. In this way, a truly peaceful world will be a world where war has been made impossible — or, at least much less likely — by a new community where people not only see themselves in their hearts as part of one human "family," but where, in (political-legal-moral) reality, they really are part of such a "family."

HOT PEACE AND COLD PEACE

One way of clearing up the confusion over terms is to define types of peace and war. Thus, there can be hot war, cold war, cold peace, and hot peace. In hot war, commonly called war, there is a condition of mutual hostility and active physical engagement through such forms as artillery, missiles, bombs, small arms fire, mortars, flamethrowers, land and sea mines, hand-to-hand combat, and the like. The aim is the destruction of the enemy or his surrender by intimidation. The object is to have a winner and loser. Nationalism reaches its zenith here.

In cold war, there is mutual hostility without actual engagement. Intimidation is the sole means of preventing hot war. This condition is characterized by propaganda, war preparations, and arms races — always at the expense of human needs. During a cold war, nationalism prevails, and the object is to have a stalemate where neither side will initiate aggression — nuclear or conventional — because of the overwhelming destructive capability of the retaliatory response.

In cold peace, there is almost a neutral view of a previous enemy. There is little mutual hostility but there is also a lack of mutually beneficial interactions aimed at developing trust, interdependence, and collaboration. There may be a longing for an enemy because nothing has replaced it as an object of national concern. In this situation, isolationism and nationalism occur simultaneously. There is no clear objective because there is no well-defined enemy. Perhaps the current U.S. military preoccupation with Iraq's Saddam Hussein and the debilitating decade of sanctions against the Iraqi people are helping to relieve this enemy deficit. The notion that "there are still dangerous people in the world" if often used to advance the cause of military preparedness and at least some momentum toward a restoration of cold war thinking and behaviour. The term "peace dividend" that expressed post cold war optimism is hardly verbalized anymore. Now we are (again) advancing ballistic missile defense — a variation of the Reagan Administration's Star Wars debacle, and an instigator of nuclear proliferation.

By contrast, hot peace involves active collaborative efforts designed to "build bridges" between and among past and present adversaries. This involves searching for common ground and the development of new non-human enemies — threats to the health and well-being of humankind and the planet. These new enemies could include human rights abuses, air and water pollution, dwindling energy resources, the destruction of the ozone layer, famine, poverty, and ignorance. Hot peace promotes and, indeed, is defined by — global interdependence, human rights, democratization, an effective United Nations, and a diminution of national sovereignty. The object is the proliferation of cooperative relations and mutually beneficial outcomes. Hot peace thinking imagines peace and the abolition of war.

Education's real, most important role is to built a consistency for peace among the young, says Graham Rager.

PEACE-EDUCATION/EDUCATION FOR PEACE

Peace is considered to be global and does not rest fully with the instructions set up to help bring peace. More to the point, it rests with each of us as individuals and there is some sense of inter-connectedness.

Three year old children argue and fight but it is worth pondering why conflicts develop on the playground? Is there a risk that the children may see violence as a means of revolving conflict? In a society that rushes to blame, who is responsible? Is it the child, his parents or the peer group? Is it his school or society at large? How do schools promote active, responsible citizens?

Schools have responsibilities, through their values and practices to educate for peace. They have an obligation to develop personal and intercultural understanding and tolerance. Although the more democratically run schools give students a voice in many aspects of school life, most are over reliant on the power of an hierarchy and, in doing so, may place students at the bottom of the pyramid. This runs the risk of alienation, subjugation and compliance through authority rather than through the personal values of right and wrong. International Schools, comprising students diverse in terms of mother tongue, culture, faith and background have a unique responsibility to promote inter-cultural understanding. Blessed as they are with all the resources that cultural diversity offers, as well as the bastions of privilege they tend to be, they need to have permeable walls. To be distinctively different from the surrounding communities yet open to them and empathic to the needs of the community. If we are clear about our stand for peace, there are some given below:

- adopt values and aims that demonstrate a commitment to peace;
- give students a voice in decision-making;
- emphasize the importance of equality of opportunity
- have a clear stance on behavioural norms and expectations;
- deal with conflict consistently and rigorously; and
- promote peace through the curriculum and events, projects,

community actions and most important, through inter-relationships.

One may ask how education can transform society? Actually, education may be transformational but it is a process rather than a single event and one that usually takes time. Educating youngsters is a vehicle for educating parents and challenging stereotypical attitudes.

By bringing together diverse cultural groups and developing attitudes of the cultural appreciation, schools can bring about a positive difference to society. But teachers need backing to be able to make the brave step of allowing diverse opinions in the classrooms. In India, the examination and assessment regime must be reformed. For every thing, a mutual understanding is just one aspect of building a consistency of peace. Standards and expectations need to be based on the school's ethos and values.

With all the above discussion, we are not yet clear regarding the concept of peace-education. Hence, it is essential to know its definition first.

PEACE-EDUCATION: A WORKING DEFINITION

❖ What is Peace-education?

Peace-education means to **learn about** and to **learn for peace.**

Learning about peace means obtaining knowledge and understanding of what contributes to peace, what damages it, what leads to war, what does 'peace' mean on each level anyway, what is my role in it, and how are the different levels connected?

Learning for peace means learning the skills, attitudes and values that one needs in order to contribute to peace and help maintain it. For example, this means learning to deal with conflict without the recourse to violence, learning to think creatively, learning to apply the methods of active non-violence or learning to deal with cultural differences in a constructive way.

Peace can take place within the individual This is 'inner peace' and some believe that this inner peace can be strengthened through with the **divine**. Inner peace involves peace of mind and absence of fear. Peace-education would not exist unless people throughout the world believe that world-peace is attainable through a multifaceted effort but starting with children and youth.

Since 'Education for Peace' is value oriented, peace being a value itself, the primary means to achieve this aim is a growing understanding of what are termed universal human values and the various ways and means of practicing them according to the capacities and potentialities of the learners. Human Rights education may be regarded as one of the approaches to peace-education.

If we are to spread real peace in the world, we shall have to begin with the children because they are the citizens of tomorrow as well as strong pillars of our society. It is an educational institution where the young minds are trained to understand the deeper meaning of peace. Here, a teacher is the most important person in managing a classroom, in guiding the pupils to achieve their goals and objectives and many more components like curricular, methods, materials, etc.

According to **R.D. Laing**, 'Peace-education is an attempt to respond to problems of conflict and violence ranging from the global and national to the local and personal. It is about exploring ways of creating more just and sustainable futures." [1978]

According to **Fran Schmidt** and **Alice Friedman** (1988) "Peace-education embraces the physical, emotional and social growth of children within a framework deeply rooted in traditional human values. It is based on philosophy that teaches love, compassion, trust, fairness cooperation and reverence for the human family and all life on our planet."

The basic concept embedded in the above definitions are that peace-education is a remedial measure to protect children from falling into the ways of violence in society. It tries to inculcate higher human and social values in the mind of the child. In essence, it attempts to develop a set of behavioural skills necessary for peaceful living from which the whole of humanity will benefit.

Peace-education is more effective and meaningful when it is adopted according to the social and cultural context and the needs of the country. It should be enriched by its cultural and spiritual values together with the universal human values. It should also be globally relevant.

❖ Teacher's Role In Peace-education

Information Technology provides open, quick and easy access in global-immense-bank of knowledge and information to the students. Students can get quick response of their problems regarding various fields by the subject experts and also specialists. They have many sources of information, faster media for communication, facility of collaborative learning, electronic devices, digital libraries, means of mobile-leasing, e-learning, etc. However, in the name of modernization, westernization is followed blindly and westernization is considered to be modernization by many students today. Spiritualism, morality, character, values and Indian culture is neglected badly. Better teacher-taught relationship became bitter-relationship. Dr. Kalam has said once that the teacher who loves teaching is an important asset. The whole life of teacher should be a message to the students and the teacher should make teaching as his or her mission. Education for peace, in its real sense is the pursuit of truth with the teacher in the central position who has to constantly refill and keep informed his or her mind so that the students will always look up to the teacher as a walking encyclopedia and a fountain of knowledge. Dr. Kalam once again holds that a teacher has a key to student's future. Shri Aurobindo believed that the teacher's job is to suggest and not to impose. He further adviced that the teachers should not be arbitrary, despotic, impatient and ill-tempered. By going through the above discussion, one is tempted to know about a teacher's role in peace-education, and we will discuss the same now.

There are four important roles of the teacher stated as below:

1. Firstly, the teacher needs to understand that multicultural, multi-ethnic and multi-religious problems in a society are not to be dealt with in isolation in bits and pieces of a good peace-education programme, but being interconnected with all other problems of peace and violence.
2. The teacher must be cognizant and wholly supportive of the basic nature and aims of peace-education. The teacher of peace-education in an apparently diverse society must aim at achieving a unified, peaceful society both globally and within the nation, where world citizenship is recognized and practiced.
3. The teacher should constantly keep in mind that the attainment of any aim is conditioned upon Knowledge, Volition and Action. The power needed to accomplish a peaceful world is the unification of human kind. Hence, the teacher has to act intelligently to reduce inter-religious violence; and to accomplish this, the teacher should develop qualities such as tolerance, respect of appreciation of others.

4. Development of teacher's own emotional intelligence is a must. Teachers who are high in Emotional Intelligence, are in a better position to deepen the aspect of peace in them.

It is in this connection it has been felt to give to the readers the five main domains of emotional intelligence linked with peace-education.

❖ Five Domains of Emotional Intelligence Linked with the Topic of Peace-education

(1) Knowing One's own emotions: Recognizing a feeling as it happens. One needs to know one's own feelings. For example, I recognize an inner feeling of bias or superiority towards a person from another ethnic group for what it really is, especially if I do not know the facts about that person. This can be a proud, selfish, self-centred feeling.

(2) Managing emotions: Handling our own feelings and emotions, the ability that builds self-awareness. *Example*: Instead of feeling anxious, sad, annoyed, upset, indifferent or dismissive when you realize you are prejudiced against a person, you decide to overcome such feelings by doing something constructive to deal with the problem.

(3) Motivating Oneself: Enlisting our emotions in service of a goal is essential for self-motivation, for mastery and for creativity. Emotional self-control is central to all sorts of accomplishments. Taking the example one step further, you set a firm goal for yourself — to overcome this prejudice through emotional self-control. You are determined to work towards your goal.

(4) Recognizing Emotions in Others: Empathy, another ability that builds on emotional self-awareness, is the basic skill in dealing with people. If you are empathic, you are more aware of the little signals that show what others need or want.

(5) Handling Relationships: The art of relationships is, in large part, the ability to manage emotions in others. As you learn more about his or her character, you are in a better position to assess your relationship with him or her. Following the basic of emotional intelligence, you have completed a peaceful act.

Thus, concludingly, it should be said that —

1. Educating for peace means examining and discussing our values and attitudes towards diversity, cultural differences, tolerance and human dignity.
2. Educating for peace means developing language and social interaction skills to promote peaceful relations among people, among nations and between human beings and the natural environment.
3. Educating for peace means learning to solve problems and to think critically regarding issues of conflict and violence.
4. Education for peace means promoting the development of the learner through an emphasis or understanding individual rights and also responsibilities.
5. Education for peace means to make the learner know as well as understand the elemental aspects of the environment.
6. Education for peace means helping pupils to gain an understanding of a local, national or an international conflict.
7. Education for peace means allowing the pupils to increase their knowledge about different aspects of conflict and the nature of causes and consequences.
8. Education for peace means helping the pupils to increase their awareness of the roles the new media plays in portraying events and conveying information.
9. Education for peace means to help pupils to enhance their capacity for informed civic participation.
10. Education for peace means helping pupils to gain self-awareness and thereby to gain insight into the concrete connections between the future and the present.
11. Education for peace means to understand the nature and origin of violence and its effects on both victims and preparator.
12. Education for peace means to create framework for achieving peaceful, creative societies.
13. Education for means to sharpen awareness about the existence of unpeaceful relationships between people and between nations.

14. Education for means to investigate the causes of conflict and violence embedded within perceptions, values, and attitudes of individuals as well as between political and social structure of society.
15. Education for peace means to encourage the search for alternative nonviolent skills.
16. Education for peace means to equip children and adults with personal conflict resolution skills.

❖ Process and methodology for use in peace-education programme may include the following:

1. Active learning/participative methods
2. Experiential learning
3. Dialogue
4. Self-expression
5. Story-telling and response to stories.
6. Project work focussed on identifying questions and researching answers.
7. Encouragement of use of source material.
8. Exchange with children from other cultures using their own medium.
9. Creative teaching and learning.
10. Whole school approach including all staff and links with the wider community.

❖ Contents of Theory Based Peace-education may include the following:

1. Role of value systems in religious and secular world views.
2. The ethics of science and technology.
3. History and present day struggle for justice and equality in race and gender.
4. Understanding the causes of violence and other national and international disputes.
5. The theory of conflict resolution.
6. Vision of the future.
7. Political and Social change.
8. The economics of war and oppression.

9. Human rights and citizenship.
10. Violence, war and peace-making in the media
11. Non-violence in literature and the arts.

❖ Content of Practical expressions of Peace-making for use in Peace-education may include the following topics:

1. Role of the United Nations and Non-Governmental Organizations.
2. How community groups affect peaceful change.
3. Models of peace-making, peace history — local, national and international.
4. Role of personal and community health and nutrition in a healthy society.
5. Understanding other cultures through language, customs and stories.
6. Child care.
7. Bullying and anti-bullying methods, peer-mediation and conflict resolution skills for children in the classroom.

NEED OF PEACE-EDUCATION OR NEED OF EDUCATION FOR PEACE

As educators, rather, as responsible teacher educators, we have to note and also understand that peace-education should reflect in curriculum, co-curricular activities and also in teaching methods. But, reality, what do we really experience? Today's education trains the citizens of tomorrow who became the builders of the Nation in their near future. Now a days education with all its various branches, levels, media and curricula is lagging behind to bring about a common understanding of the nation. All the levels and boards of education teach and preach the child to develop as a segregated, selfish, imbalanced, individual, thinking of his own personal benefits. He is even neglecting his family, siblings, friends and others. This develops negative feelings among the individuals and children are facing anxieties, frustration, depression, phobias etc. At this sensitive juncture, peace-education is the only remedy which plays an important role in bringing up global understanding. The modern world is shrinking. The new revolution invention in science and technology have brought the countries together. No doubt, but side by side a competitive feeling among human is also taking place. The developed nations are dominating other developed nations; and this has decreased the atmosphere of peace. Distinction of caste, creed, colour, nationalism, suspicion and jealously among the people has resulted in violence and terror. Therefore, it is essential that we should try to make our students feel that they are the members of one world; and thereby, they must also be encouraged to practice tolerance and respect for others.

Because if the above said facts, it is felt that peace-oriented education is the need of the hour. Education shapes the society and society guides the process of education. It is peace-education which serves as a powerful means to change

❖ Aims of Peace-education/Objectives of Peace-education

Education must blossom human excellence by the introduction of peace-education. Learning how to work together, play together and share decision-making, create and produce together and work through conflicts are the requisite competencies which the citizens of today must possess. This will be done definitely through the inculcation of peace-education programmes in schools. It is the teacher's training colleges that should help their teacher-educators learn how to make their judicious use collectively rather than with selfish motives. For this, it is needless to state that the profession of teachers should never be reduced to a trade. It is a calling of vocation, a mission. Hence, it is the duty of teachers to make pupils good citizens of the new democracy. They must impart to the students zest for new experiences and love for adventure in knowledge. Honesty of thought, speech and written words is like a jewel.

Based on the above discussion, it will be now easy for us to lay out the aims or objectives of peace-education which runs as follows —

❖ The Aim of Education for Peace

The aims of EP stated by UNESCO (as quoted by Kekkonen, 1985) are the following:

- The stimulation of children's emotional and intellectual development.
- The development of certain characteristics like responsibility for and sympathy for the under-privileged and the oppressed.

- The development of critical thinking.
- The development of the ability to work within a group.
- The development of the ability to make sound decisions and value-judgments based on rational thinking.
- The creation of a learning culture and of the notion that learning is a life-long process.

Hicks (1988) make a valuable distinction between skills, attitudes and knowledge. From this, one can clearly deduce that EP is a process that stresses both content and method. The aims that Hicks stipulate are:

Skills: Critical thinking, co-operation, empathy, assertiveness, conflict resolution, political literacy.

Attitudes: Self -respect, respect for others, ecological concern, open-mindedness, vision, commitment to justice.

Knowledge: Conflict, peace, war, justice, power, gender, race, environment.

Bjerstedt (August 1992) identified several areas as priority aims based on international survey. These aims are:

- Global perspectives
- The ability to generate alliterative visions
- Inter-cultural awareness
- Insight into social injustice
- The willingness to work for a more just world
- Acceptance of an ethic of human rights
- Willingness to work for a peaceful world
- An ethic of non-violence
- Insight into the consequences of violence-based solutions to problems.
- The ability to evaluate historical developments critically
- Involvement in the international community
- Ecological of responsibilities
- Assertiveness
- Awareness of prejudices
- Striving for equality

1. To develop a sort of awareness in the pupils about self and society.

2. To inculcate the concept of peace in the minds of the pupils for self-discipline, self-reliance, truth, honesty, etc.
3. To provide opportunities for children for positive social attitude.
4. To make teacher-trainees sensitive for the establishment of peace in classroom situation.
5. To provide awareness regarding the concept of education for peace.
6. To build, to maintain and to store relationships at all levels of human interaction.
7. To develop in the minds of the pupils positive approaches towards dealing with conflicts — from personal to national and then to international.
8. To create in pupils a healthy self-environment both physically and emotionally that nurture each individual.
9. To help pupil to establish a self-world based on justice and human rights.
10. To assist pupils to build a sustainable environment and protect it from exploitation and war.
11. Main aim of peace-education will be to make teachers sensitive to the value-needs of pupils and their full adjustment to society of future.

It has been rightly suggested by the National Policy document that the future teacher is the hope of India's regeneration through education. He has to mobilize peace-education through his lessons and his lectures in classroom social service and community development programmes. He is nation-builder and destiny-maker of the future generations. As it is well know that —

- Good teachers make good schools
- Good Schools make good students
- Good Students make good citizens
- Good citizens make good nations.

Thus, from the above discussion it becomes quite clear that peace-education is based on a philosophy that teaches non-violence, compassion, love, cooperation, problem-solving, critical thinking, trust, fairness and reverence for human family and all life on our planet.

No doubt, peace-education leads to peaceful living!

In spite of the above discussion, concludingly, following lines are added —

The main aim of peace-education is to conscientize the learners towards their total situations in which they live. Due to awareness about their oppressive and exploitative conditions, they become capable of initiating to eliminate structural violence which is the cause of physical violence. Magnus Haavelsrud says that conscientization efforts would create political forces which would be instrumental in the struggle for social justice on global as well as local levels, including changes in the formal educational system. The aim of peace-education is also to assure the creation of culture of peace. Culture of peace protects all including those who are afflicted with poverty, sickness, bereavement, unemployment, imprisonment, exile and oppression, and on the whole it protects the masses from all types of exploitation. According to Chirstoph Wulf, the aim of peace-education is to incorporate into the educational process the dangers posed to human life and human social life by war, violence, poverty, and oppression. Personal Liberation is the final aim of peace-education as it is observed by Robin Richardson. The aim of peace-education is to make everyone be friends with correcting genuine injustice or conflicts of interest between them as it is believed by Adam Curle. Betty Reardon says that the purpose of peace-education is to provide knowledge to be applied to the problem of reforming and/or restructuring present human society to make it more just and less violent.

Here special mention is made on the efforts of Mabel Aranha, who has been involved in peace-education in India since 1986. She developed a peace-education syllabus after extensive discussions with teachers for Classes V-VII. This was tried out with children over a period of three years. The objectives of the programme were:

(*i*) To instill a desire for peace and harmony and a dislike for war and violence,

(*ii*) To promote an understanding of co-existence and interdependence.

(*iii*) To foster an appreciation of differences between people of various religions, states and countries.

She also attempted in 1992 to introduce peace-education at the Bachelor of Education Degree Course in a progressive teacher training college. She created a positive attitude and developed a comprehensive resource on peace-education for the college. The new syllabus for the Bachelor of Education degree programme of the University of Madras has introduced Human Rights as an Elective paper from the academic year 2003-2004.

Later Ake Bjerstedt surveyed the situation of Peace-education in different countries. He interviewed several leading Educationists of different countries of the world. He interviewed Ms. Anima Bose of India, who voiced her concern over the absence of Peace-education not included in the curriculum of mainstream education. However, she felt that in a country where Gandhi was born, there are several universities that include some aspects of Peace-education in an inter-disciplinary way and the schools also have Peace-education in an indirect way.

Therefore, Peace-education is the need of the hour and women have a significant role in fostering it to children at various levels. Let us live a peaceful life and transmit peace and love to the world through children.

Concludingly, it may be said that teaching peace is not restricted to a particular school or context using a specific methodology or practice. A culture of teaching peace recognizes varied and diverse learning environments where students encounter opportunities to refine their notion of peace. Nature hikes, punk concerts, trips to the library and flying a kite are some of the activities outside the classroom, which 'count' as peace-education. Science teachers can teach peace by promoting environmental awareness. Foreign language teachers can read or translate primary source texts from the target language which detail experiences in personal, national and global peacemaking efforts. Physics classes can learn about the subatomic exchange of matter and energy, which binds to all humans to one another. Themes of peace and justice can be infused in every content subject so that peace is pervasive in the curriculum.

A culture of teaching peace can also begin in unconventional places. In prisons and juvenile detention facilities in the United States, a curriculum called Solutions to Violence is impacting the incarcerated youths and adults in a positive way. Death Row inmates have begun teaching the class, and graduates proudly display their diploma stating that they have read the likes of Tolstoy, Gandhi, Merton and King. A culture of teaching peace is beginning to take hold in the places reserved for the most violent criminals. Students of peace in any environment can learn the principles of conflict resolution and internalize the messages in Thich Nhat Hanh's vast literature.

❖ How to Educate for Peace

Education for Peace must consider not only the content but teaching methods and strategies to make content effective and meaningful. We are to teach not only ABOUT peace, but to teach FOR peace and IN peace as well.

We can educate for peace by formal and informal methods:

❖ Formal methods:

1. Direct teaching
2. Formal lesson plans
3. Hidden curriculum

❖ Informal methods:

1. Assembly programmes
2. Community singing
3. Activities

Let us discuss about the Formal methods:

(1) Direct-Teaching

Here, use of lecture method may be used in the classroom to inform and instruct on the contents and themes of peace. Secondly, use of discussion method may be adopted to discuss about the themes by using newspaper clippings, T.V. shows, books and films.

(2) Formal Lesson Plans

Here, four principles are to be kept in mind while teaching for peace:

(*i*) The choice of specific learning activities to educate for peace depends on the needs of the pupils and the objectives must be formulated according to these needs.

(*ii*) Motivation must be used at the beginning of each lesson as well as appropriate points of the lesson by pointing out that education for peace upholds life and universal principles of truth.

(*iii*) Include the various dimensions of the pupil — cognitive, affective and behavioural aspect of personality.

(*iv*) Make peace an end as well as a process through a relaxed classroom, active listening and cooperation.

(3) Hidden Curriculum

The hidden curriculum is defined as that structure and mileu in which the written curriculum finds expression.

Peace-education is best taught through the hidden curriculum, which reveals the values and attitudes of the school community. If peace-education is an exercise in building tolerance, understanding, cooperation and a willingness to accept differences among people, then the first place to look all these values is within the school itself. Schools should be vehicles of positive change, prejudice, verbal violence and physical violence should not be a part of its structure. Schools should reflect what society believes to be good rather than what is undesirable.

❖ Ways of promoting peace through the hidden curriculum:

— Clean and attractive buildings and grounds.

— Flexible seating.

— Multicultural environment through activities like celebration of festivals.

— Using democratic decision making.

— Encouraging team work and group exercises.

— Avoiding verbal, physical and psychological violence in the classroom.

— Evaluating according to the development of each student with his past performance and not with respect to each other.

— Keeping the school open for use of the community.

— Letting parents and the community communicate with the school administrators and staff.

Let us now discuss about Informal Methods.

• In the informal method, use of assembly and activities are seen. Most schools have a general assembly programme at the beginning of the day. The students are in a favourable frame of mind and are receptive to ideas at this time. Groups of students from the classes involved in peace-education can conduct the assembly on themes related to peace. The programme can include:

(*a*) A prayer related to the theme.

(*b*) A brief explanation of the theme.

(*c*) A hymn or song best suited to the theme.

(*d*) Readings from newspapers with comments or a poem based on the themes or a skit.

The activities at the assembly are a good means of counteracting the forces of communalism, regionalism and religious bigotry. When children realise that there can be a form of worship common to all and yet it does not impringe on their own beliefs, it is possible to build up a climate of religious respect and appreciation.

Since peace is a universal value, sometimes pupils are asked to collect various symbols of peace a day before the discussion and display them on the notice board. At some other time, a teacher encourages pupils to design other symbols in groups and hang them up in the class.

So too, many a time, the teacher adopts a policy of 'Let us do it together' and helps pupils experience through cooperative behaviour. This is how pupils think how they can cooperate to make the world better.

Some such similar activities can be thought of by the teacher for peace-education purpose. Concludingly, it may be said that as it is, our syllabus is content heavy and teachers really have a very difficult time trying to complete the topics. Hence, it is suggested that 10 minutes must be kept aside once or twice a week during the year for different types of activities to be conducted by them (pupils). If the entire work is well-planned, most of the teachers will find it easy to complete the task undertaken.

The children's room in the library should be supplied with books and pictures about the children of other nations, and such others as will give children a sense of the unity of mankind and the interdependence of nations. International Mind Alcoves for children to interest them in "their friends of other lands" have recently been started by the Carneigic Endowment, and are proving popular. An attractive feature can be made of children's books of other nations by arranging them to suggest a trip around the edge of a world map or a map can be bring on the wall behind the table of books, with the names of the books about each country printed in the margin.

❖ Key Values In Educating for Peace

1. It realises the necessity of prayer.
2. It begins with self-transformation, rethinking and redirecting of our lives.

3. It allows for and encourages growth of compassion and insight into other people's lives and their right to human dignity.
4. It develops critical awareness and understanding of the world and its dilemmas.
5. It recognises the reality of conflict, tension, aggression and violence as part of life and seeks creative ways of growing.
6. It creates awareness of unjust and oppressive structures — national and international.
7. It sees peace as fundamental for human survival and well-being of the earth's ecosystem and works for the oneness of mankind by diminishing the threats of war and nuclear armaments.
8. It motivates towards constructive social change and a new world order.

❖ Values and Attitudes Required for Peace-Education

— Respect for others regardless of race, gender, age, nationality, class, sexuality, appearance, political belief, physical or mental ability.

— Empathy — a willingness to understand the views of others from their standpoint.

— A belief that individuals and groups of people can make for positive change.

— Appreciation of and respect for diversity.

— Self esteem — accepting the intrinsic value of oneself.

— Commitment to social justice, equity and nonviolence

— Concern for the environment and understanding of our place in the eco-system commitment to equality.

❖ Concluding Remarks

Peace-education should start aiming at the targeted audience at the elementary level. The mode of teaching may be through the audio-video cassettes, staging plays, showing films and conducting weekly classes by peace-educators in mobile vans. The activities must be aimed on the aspect of 'Learning By Doing' — whether it is individual activity or group activity. There must be proper allocation of the financial resources for implementing Peace-education Programmes; and these should be conducted periodically. Most important thing to note is that pupils need to be motivated for attending peace-education activities regularly, and these activities should be such which interest them. In addition to routine class-activities, the schools should invite experts from various non-governmental organization, during every academic year, to conduct workshops on several issues pertaining to life-skills which eventually aim at understanding and actualising peace.

❖ Evaluation

Peace-education programme in educating pupils and the school community as a whole can be evaluated through the presence of the following indicators —

At the personal level, evidence of:

1. Tolerance
2. Equality
3. Respect
4. Effective communication
5. Openness
6. Reconciliation
7. Solidarity.

At the classroom level, evidence of:

1. Recognition of diversity and disparity
2. Open and respectful student/staff relationships.
3. Co-operative group work
4. Seeking peaceful resolutions.

At the School level, evidence of:

1. Fair school rules
2. Appropriate educational activities related to peace
3. Supportive pastoral care
4. A secure and non-threatening climate
5. Representation
6. Staff development Programme relevant to Peace-education.

At the community level, evidence of:

1. Service programs
2. Demonstrating leadership

3. Outreach programs
4. Awareness of problems and contributions to solutions.

While academic discourse on the subject of peace-education has increasingly recognized the more holistic approach to peace-education, a review of field-based subjects reveals that three variations of peace-education are more common. These are —

(*i*) Conflict resolution training,

(*ii*) Democracy education, and

(*iii*) Human rights education.

(i) Peace-education as Conflict Resolution Training

Peace-education programmes centred on conflict resolution focus typically on the social-behavioural systems of conflict; training individuals to resolve inter-personal disputes through techniques of negotiation and [peer] meditation. Learning to manage anger, "fight-fair" and improve communication through skills such as listening, turntaking, identifying needs and separating facts from emotions, constitute the main elements of these programmes.

In general, approaches of this type aim to alter beliefs, attitudes, and behaviours from negative to positive attitude towards conflict as a basis for preventing violence.

(ii) Peace-education as Democracy Education

Peace-education programmes centred on democracy education typically focus on the political processes associated with conflict, and postulate that with an increase in democratic participation, the likelihood of societies resolving conflict through violence and war decreases. At the same time "a democratic society needs the commitment of citizens who accept the inevitability of conflict as well as necessity for tolerance." [US Development of State, the Culture of Democracy]. Thus, programmes of this kind attempt to foster a conflict-positive orientation in the community by training learners to view conflict as a platform for creativity and growth.

The aim is thus to produce responsible citizens who will hold their governments accountable to the standards of peace, primarily through adversarial processes, by assuming the role of the citizen that chooses, makes decisions, takes positions and respects the opinions of others. Based on the assumption that democracy decreases the likelihood of violence and war, it is assumed that these are the same skills necessary for creating a culture of peace.

(iii) Peace-education as Human-rights Education

Peace-education programmes centred on raising awareness of human rights typically focus at the level of policies that humanity ought to adopt in order to move closer to a peaceful global community. The aim is to engender a commitment among people to a vision of structural peace in which all individual members of the human race can exercise their personal freedoms and be legally protected from violence, oppression and indignity.

Approaches of this type familiarizes with the international convenants and declaration of the United Nations System, train learners to recognize violations of the Universal Declaration of Human Rights; and promote tolerance, solidarity autonomy and self-affirmation at the individual as well as collective levels.

Human Rights education faces continual elaboration, a sufficient theory-practice gap and frequent challenge as to its validity.

To prevent these outcomes, many such programmes are now combined with assets of conflict resolution and democracy education school of thought, along with training in non-violent action.

Now, the question that jumps up like a boomrang is, 'what is the contribution of teacher-educators?' Hence, let us discuss it in brief as follows —

In fact, the teacher-educators have much to contribute to the development of quality amongst the teachers. It is really high time that they understand their role rather than simply criticize the system in the name of NCTE. If they do not contribute, their status will be one of irrelevance. Hence, they ought to respond to both empirical as well as pedagogical levels. [*Liston* et al. 2008]

(1) The first thing is that they will have to accept the existing realities of the world. Privatization has entered educational system and they cannot deny it at any cost. A large number of men and women aspire to get degree or diplomas in teacher education to join teaching jobs. The existing teacher education colleges cannot accommodate all the aspirants. The nation at such a juncture will have to depend on private participation in education system of the country. Teacher education programmes in India have never been based on demand and supply phenomenon.

There has always been a good number of participants who never joined teaching after earning a degree or diploma in education. It has generally been observed that objective of many women in getting admission to teacher-education programmes has been to earn a certificate for future employment. Many a women join teaching after a decade of getting progressional degree in wake of their personal or family problems. In such a situation, there is a need to draft teacher-education courses that have totally specialized knowledge, specialized skills and inherent code of ethics.

(2) Secondly, the teacher-educators will have to delve on specialised skills that add quality to the professional functioning, Such skills mean having hard, technical expertise along with softer interpersonal capabilities. Skills of quality teaching and quality assessment are most desired. Quality teaching skills involve the process of making students work hard and become independent learner. For example, posing a problem before the learners and helping them find solutions to these problems is a skill and such skills need to be developed in the teacher trainees. Similarly, the teacher trainees have to be trained in quality assessment procedure. This type of assessment requires the trainees to assess the students with respect to their thinking process and learning styles. In the same manner, the skills related to feed back have to be developed amongst future teachers so that the feedback is accepted open-mindedly by the students and they improve upon.

Almost all the learners from the World's oldest universities have always evinced an interest in the topic of 'peace'. In fact, peace first became a subject of discussion in the years immediately following the American Civil War [1861-1865]. In fact, the First World War changed the Western attitude towards war; and after the Second World War, the United Nations was established to ensure a peaceful future. Truely speaking, the preamble to the United Nations Charter, the United Nations was established to "save succeeding generation from the scourge of war", "to reaffirm faith in the ..... dignity and worth of the human person (and) in the equal rights of men and women," "to promote social progress and better standards of life in large freedom..."

Peace-education thus developed as a means to achieve these goals.

Global awareness has become peace-education in action; and educator focus on fostering international and intercultural understanding, teaching respect and tolerance, for those who are different. Scholars, activists and reformers use peace-education as a way to bring harmony among groups of people, primarily through schools and classrooms.

❖ Concluding Remarks

While there are many definitions of peace-education [which we have already soon], the field is generally considered multidisciplinary and includes a focus on peace studies, social justice, economic well being [meeting basic needs], political participation [citizenship], non-violence, conflict resolution, disarmament, human rights and concern for the environment. Peace-educators at various times have engaged with additional areas of inquiry including feminism, global education and cultural diversity. Peace educators have long advocated for the recognition of the worth of others who may be different, who may speak other languages and yet share the fact of this fragile planet, Earth.

Peace ideas, peace studies and peace activities of peace-educators of the world, have been consolidated in the form of papers, research-reports, peace-addresses and peace-messages, peace-news, peace-education directory in the volumes of papers in Peace-education.

Peace-education is the process of promoting knowledge, skills, attitudes and values needed to bring about behaviour changes that will enable children, youth and adults to prevent conflict and violence.

A Peace-education is an attempt to respond to problems of conflict and violence on scales ranging from the global and national to the local and personal. It is about exploring ways of creating more just and sustainable futures. — *R. D. Laing* (1978)

Peace-education is holistic. It embraces the physical, emotional, intellectual, and social growth of children within a framework deeply rooted in traditional human values. It is based on philosophy that teaches love, compassion, trust, fairness, co-operation and reverence for the human family and all life on our beautiful planet.

— *Fran Schmidt and Alice Friedman* (1988)

The basic concepts embedded in the above definitions are that peace-education is a remedial measure to protect children from falling into the ways of violence in society. It aims at the total development of the child. It tries to inculcate higher human and social values in the mind of the child. In essence, it attempts to develop a set of behavioural skills necessary for peaceful living and peace-building from which the whole of humanity will benefit.

The word peace has a broad meaning. In fact, it is an umbrella term that covers a wide range and shades of meanings. Therefore in order to make it a clear and unambiguous base for any educational purpose, it has to be interpreted as something that students can learn and change their ways of behaviour both as individuals and groups for a better future. The outcome of such learning should be observed and evaluated objectively.

To live in the true sense, we need peace in every way. It provides the atmosphere, space and nourishment essential to grow towards human perfection. However, we have to frankly accept the fact that we still lack a great deal of understanding of what peace really is. Hence there is considerable negligence and confusion in the field. Practically people tend to define peace according to their own preferred perspectives. Consider the following interpretations:

Economics: Peace is the eradication of poverty. It is the economic wellbeingness of people.

Politics: Peace is the outcome of democracy. Peace results from good governance.

Anti-military: Stop war and there is peace.

Law: Peace is law and order.

Social harmony: Resolve conflicts between diverse groups. Integrate such groups together through the distribution of justice.

On the above said facts, let us say that we as teachers, must carry the torch of Indian way of peaceful living and for each one to live and grow.

In the words of Betty Reardon, "Peace-education would provide knowledge to be applicable to the problems of reforming and restructuring the present conflicts and violence in human society to make it peaceful, unified and violence-free."

Peace-education is a broader discipline which can be applicable to Environment education, Human right education, International education are associated with Peace-education. Peace-education deals with conflicts arising out of aggression or war situations and also arising out of injustice, exploitations and violation of Human rights. Peace-education creates a culture of peace, helping to build non-violent education systems for the nation building. The peace-education can involve everyone such as academic administrators, academicians, researchers, teachers, students, parents and the community. It promotes an awareness of reciprocations through dialogs, evidence of non-violent, and a means to achieving personal peace in the individual's minds.

By teaching Peace-education, pupils —

(*i*) gain an understanding of local, national or international conflicts,

(*ii*) increase their knowledge about different aspects of conflict and the nature of causes and consequences,

(*iii*) increase awareness of roles, the news media plays in portraying events and conveying information,

(*iv*) practice skills in conflict analysis and critical thinking,

(*v*) increase their ability to filter information presented in the media,

(*vi*) practice skills of teamwork and communication,

(*vii*) enhance their capacity for informed civic participation.

Peace-education is indeed a great idea to work on in a school. There are few problems, however, that need to be discussed if a school is determined to produce a generation of peace-citizens.

1. First, the structure of education is replete with an unsaid hierarchy. At the top, it has mainstream teaching and learning meant for passing exams under the ambit of formal education. This is where most of the lessons that children learn in the workshops are contradicted. The idea of peace is not evenly distributed in the structure of education.
2. Secondly, the vision, insights and tools and techniques the children learn are not always appreciated by the outside world.
3. Workshops by experts may be too regimented and rationalised in terms of the means and the end to be taken into consideration, the meaningful irrationality of the learners.

If peace-education is to have the necessary impact, it is imperative to recall Prof. Krishna Kumar. "The unpredictable outcomes of learning are far more important than the ones we can predict and plan for. This is so because the crisis caused by violence and conflict in the human world is far deeper and vast than any rational plan can resolve. Only miracles can, if we let them happen, as they do quite often, eventlessly." Hopefully, schools pursuing peace-education will evolve a pedagogic structure that can greet miraculous developments of the learners.

❖ Significance of Peace-education

Peace-education, is in essence a good education which should be based an positive and rewarding human relationship. Peace-attempted education should attempt to reduce the willingness to use violence in individuals and to remove the infrastructures which cause violence in human relations at all levels of society and among nations. Different strategies are silent-sitting, drama, role-play, story-telling, discussion, some exemplar ideas, maintaining a diary, examinations, and assessment issues. A teacher's role is crucial always.

Peace is important because we need a better world for our next generation. Peace is important because we enjoy the beliefs of the latest technological and scientific advancement only in times of peace. Peace-education and peace curriculum should be based on the thoughts of eminent peace-activists. "Avoiding war is the work of politics, establishing peace is the work of education" should be one of the basic tenets of education curriculum.

Peace-education is really a very important part of our educational system where schools can:

(*i*) develop a more humanistic approach management,

(*ii*) improve human relations between teacher and student, between teacher and teacher, and between student and student,

(*iii*) build healthy emotional development in students,

(*iv*) facilitate socialization through participation in cooperative learning activities,

(*v*) improve students discipline and moral behaviour,

(*vi*) develop creativity both in students as well as teachers,

(*vii*) improve standard of quality teaching and learning. One should not forget the saying —

"Better to light a candle than curse the darkness!"

❖ Challenges for Peace-education

- Peace-education faces such challenges not-withstanding its qualitative and quantitative expansion of the 1980 and 1990. In many respect, one of the institutional problems of peace-education is that it has no strong international academic infrastructure like many of the other disciplines.

- A second disadvantage is that there are very few institutes which focus their research and training activities on peace-education.
- A third problem relates to the conceptual framework of peace-education.

What is peace-education? What is the language of peace-education? How do different cultures interpret peace-education? What new philosophical basis is required for the peace-educating? What new philosophical basis is required for the future of peace-education? The future of peace-education as a philosophy needs fresh rethinking in particular in relation to the following areas of study:

- The evaluation of peace-education and its place in education programmes and societies;
- The theoretical and pedagogical approaches to peace-education;
- Peace-education and value-based perspectives;
- Research and curriculum development;
- The concept of peace-education in the various cultures;
- Peace-education in science and technology;
- Peace-education and formal systems of education.

Entire learning in the school must never be done by traditional lectures, but by working in the field with practical jobs and by participation is various games and other activities during the course. Learning should never be just isolated to schools; it can happen anywhere, at any time. We, as teachers, can try to prepare our children and youth to meet the challenges that they face today and bring about a positive transformation towards a culture of peace.

❖ Conclusion

Peace-education must safeguard its territory. Traditionally it has been too generous in allocating space for the other disciplines to adjust their requirements within a general philosophy of peace. Similarly, peace educators have found it comfortable to adapt knowledge into peace kits and programmes and present this as a coherent whole. In my view, the future of peace-education depends on our ability to create a sort of scientific symbiosis.

The old traditional paradigm sees peace as external phenomena. The new paradigm considers peace as external, as well as internal phenomena. The thesis of the old paradigm is therefore taken into account and finds their place in an integrated whole in which three main aspects play a leading role namely: knowledge, democracy and culture. Knowledge is an outer energy which originates form basic needs and can grow up to self-realization. It determines both personal and social development and demands organization, flexibility, accountability and responsibility. The acquisition of knowledge can be interpreted as a flow parting from needs to self-fulfillment, more or less cycles and re-cycles or information, evolution and action. The second area is related to the study of democracy. Here, three basic principles have been identified, namely dignity, equality, and mutual respect. Peace-education has been traditionally associated to these values and good number of books exists on how to approach pedagogically these there important issues. The third grouping focuses on culture an moral solidarity. It is not knowledge in general but culture as the refinement of mind, moral and taste. How can peace-education promote solidarity through handicrafts, agriculture, economics, music, art; religious beliefs, tradition, language and story telling.

♣♣♣

2

ANALYSIS OF INDIAN SOCIETY

Human beings have been dreaming and thinking about impossible, unrealizable, and realizable ideals since their existence. "Only those who can see the invisible can do the impossible," was rightly said by Bernard Lown, President of International Physicians for the Prevention of Nuclear War, which was awarded the Nobel Peace Prize in 1985. Frank Manuel having faith on man's capacity pointed out, "The creature, it seems, could not stop dreaming even as he stood beneath the gallows of the atomic launching pad". Humans have never been fully satisfied with the existing knowledge and practices. They always aspire for new knowledge which help them to create new culture and civilization for building a better society. Hence Einstein said, "Imagination is better than knowledge". So, then Director-General of UNESCO Federico Mayor advised, "To increase the power of the imagination and strengthen human desire to go ever further, is to equip mankind to face reality and respond to the unexpected". And their remarks and advices are true because all discoveries, inventions, creations of new culture and civilizations are the results of imagination of strong, determined, and perpetually learning and transcending minds of the people.

It is not right to say that imagination is absent from scientific work and scientist is merely supposed to lift the cover, which hides a pre-established truth; because, imagination is a must in the work of scientists as well as in the work of creative persons, and both create on the basis of their imagination.

The then President of Indian Republic Dr. A.P.J. Abdul Kalam — a distinguished scientist — has written in a poem, "Dreams float on an impatient wind, a wind that wants to create a new order — an order of strength and thundering of fire." Hence, he advised — "Learn to dream. Let them be meaningful big dreams; and live to fulfill those dreams." It is also true to say that our land need not be a land only of dreams, but it should be a goal to realise a paradise on earth.

A good paradise on earth, in the real sense of the term means nothing but a good society with good civilization. Civilizations of many generations were produced by infinite labour of creative people, priests of learning and prophets of different nations. Their ideas, principles, theories, laws, formulas, preaching and practices for which they were humiliated, tortured and killed, are, in fact the real founder members of global civilization. Dr. Young Seek Choue has also written — "Human Civilization is not a product of capricious chance but the monumental achievement of those, who, despite dark shadows cast over the world, tried to see the bright side of human life and worked ceaselessly to achieve something worthwhile. The heritage of human-civilization is the monument of lofty ideals of man."

In fact, mostly rulers, heads of different sects, classroom teachers and common masses do not dare to dream. Hence their stereotype thinking and practices had made civilizations sick, violent, oppressive and intolerant. In this regard, one may refer to the following books and the relevant papers: *Civilizations and its Discontents* (1953) of **Freud**, *The Sane Society* (1956) of **Erich Fromm,** *Sickness of Civilization* (1964) of **Radhakamal Mukerjee,** *Madness and Civilization* (1965) of **Michel Foucault,** *Madness in Society* (1968) of **George Rosen**; "Social Conditioning of Mental Illness" (*Sachitra Aurveda*, Jan. 1969), "Social Environment and Mental Diseases" (*Social Welfare*, June 1970), and "Mental Illness as Social Deviance" (*Indian Journal of Social Research,* August 1970) of **Surya Nath Prasad.**

It was Immanuel Kant (Education, 1960) who had analysed the difficulties involved in the societies gave advice regarding the education of children —

Children ought to be educated, not for the present, but for a possibly improved condition of man in the future; that is, in a manner which is adopted to the idea of humanity and the whole destiny of man.... Parents usually educate their children merely in such a manner that, however bad the world may be, they may adapt themselves to its present conditions. But they ought to give them an education so much better than this, that a better condition of things may thereby be brought about in the future. Here, however, we are met by two difficulties — (*a*) parents usually only care that their children make their way in the world, and (*b*) sovereigns looks upon their subjects merely as tools for their own purposes.... Neither have as their aim the universal good and the perfection to which man is destined, and for which he has also a natural disposition. But the basis of a scheme of education must be cosmopolitan. And is, then the idea of the universal good harmful to us as individuals? Never! For though it may appear that something must be sacrificed by this idea, an advance is also made towards what is best even for the individual under his present conditions. And then what glorious consequences follow!

In fact, seeds — physical, vital, mental, intellectual and spiritual — in all men and women are omnipresent. And their integral manifestation throughout life is education. The horizon of education is limitless. Hence education is also omnipresent. This lifelong perpetual integral education would be for deprived existing peoples in compensatory form, and for innocent coming generation in original form.

In view of Jacques Delors, Chairman of the International Commission on Education for the twenty-first Century, learning throughout life is the heartbeat of society. He considers education, which is based on four pillars, *viz.* learning to know, learning to do, learning to live together and learning to be as proposed by the Commission, is the necessary Utopia (Learning: The Treasure Within, 1996). But Federico Mayor, then Director-General of UNESCO added two more pillars of education learning to undertake, and learning to dare (1996). The author of this editorial also supplemented two more pillars of education; learning to share, and learning to be just to make the roof of education stable (Prasad, 2003). Delors says that humankind sees in education an indispensable asset in attempts to attain the ideal of peace, freedom and social justice .

❖ A Global Call

What do we call them who crucified Christ, poisoned to death to Socrates, burned John Huss at stake, burnt Bruno, thrown Plato into prison, forced Galileo to recant, and assassinated Mahatma Gandhi, and also those who are oppressing, exploiting and killing people? They may certainly be called ignorant in the words of Christ. Hence they needed education, they need education of, about and for man. For this, we require 100 years to grow man in view of Confucius. However, to execute the plan expeditiously to grow man hidden in all men and women, we must give rein of governance in the hands of creators, thinkers, true scientists, real saints and sages who are perfect of their ideals, and very much ready to translate them into reality to the benefit of all. They may plan, facilitate and execute better without any prejudice and discrimination including the policies of lifelong perpetual man-making education for all and in all *i.e.,* peace-education which would be core-curriculum in all formal educations, and it would be beyond campus education also. If these creative utopians keep themselves aloof from the activities of their respective governments, they will be bound to suffer alongwith the masses. Perhaps this would be the reason to Plato who warned centuries ago. "The penalty that goodmen pay for refusing to take part in government is to live under the government of badmen." But now we may say that governments of all States must offer honourably the oughtopian creative persons of their respective nations to join and take responsibilities in the governance; or such persons should contest the election, and all sections of the society: parents, teachers, preachers, and even persons of ruling class and bureaucracy should elect them; as the political situations in the state would be. No doubt, under the governance of these creative people, planning and execution of education of man for all and in all would create self-governed people being perpetually learning, creating and transcending. And this type of man-making education would create ideal men and women for sustainable development and peace to all. Certainly, education for all and in all is an education which must be realized to make society — a society of ought-to-be a reality.

❖ Cultivating a Democratic Spirit

We human beings are endowed with the ability of thinking and imagination. Hence, we must try to achieve that society, which is a desirable society, where we can live like true human beings, by setting up the goal we ought to pursue successfully.

We all have to be aware that we are living in the age of democracy. Accordingly, we all have to launch a global movement for peace-making by upholding the universality of freedom, equality and co-prosperity of all the people and by respecting the rights of all the stages and sovereignty. The utility of modern war is so drastically limited by the advancement of the destructive power of weapon systems that a victory in war is really meaningless!

❖ Reconstruction of Human Society

It is obvious that the limit of the contemporary materialistic civilization which has really brought a neglect of human dignity; and a blind belief in the advantage of technology, is responsible today for the alienation of human beings and the lack of humanity!

As a result of the science — technological revolution and information revolution — the world has become truely a global village which is making the world a "sphere of simultaneous life," and deepening the independent relationship of the people.

In view of these revolutionary changes, the things of the past such as exclusionary nationalism, ideological beliefs, and hegemonism are no longer relevant forces or factors that determine the world affairs,

Along with these revolutionary changes, we see also the spread and universalization of democratic ideals and institutions, the universal recognition of the necessity of respecting human dignity, and the rising of humanitarian consciousness, The strengthening of democracy, human dignity, and humanitarianism are becoming definite factors that will make our human society a truly peaceful, humane, and welfare-oriented cultural society.

Due to the qualitative and quantitative increase of international cooperation, exchanges, transaction, interdependence, and mutual penetration in economic, cultural, social, and scientific-technological fields, the existing international system will have to transform into a fundamentally new system that will be instrumental in globalization, democratization, humanization and "welfarization" of the whole world in order to facilitate the realization of a truly meaningful global society to all the peoples of the world.

Only when we have achieved such a global system in response to the changes that require a new spirit for the forthcoming new millennium, we will become true world citizens as well as bona fide members of the human family living in one global village with common goals, common norms and common tasks. Nevertheless human beings today are so overwhelmed by materialistic inclinations and so preoccupied by the advancement of science and technology that we have now a society where materials are more valued than men and where men are downgraded by science and technology. Thus, we have created a society lacking humility. Materials, science, technology, institutions, and organizations are all created by men, and thus, they must be the means to serve mankind. We should never let ourselves be dominated by what we have created.

Humanity has the responsibility to transform educating instruments into laboratories of the spirit of peace, a crucible in which to form a new mentality of peace. The permanent conditions for the peaceful world can be created only through education. Therefore, the importance, effectiveness and needs for peace must be present during all stages of person's formation.

'Peace is possible for life at al stages and it is up to man to choose his destiny or to suffer from the horrors of war. Today mankind is at the cross-road where he has to choose with courage, determination and imagination. — *Federics Mayor*

❖ How very true!

Violence is emerging in an unprecedental manner in human society. It is really sad to realise that we live in an era of unprecedental violence in the form of terrorism, war, crimes, injustice and exploitation amidst a seemingly outward development enjoyed by a few. There is so much disorder and confusion in the society; and majority of mankind are struggling for bare survival and living in stark poverty! This confusion in the society is affecting the children's innocent minds. They naturally absorb the spirit of violence in the atmosphere and will soon grow to be the next generation of perpetuators of violence! Hence, a need to nurture peace in the hearts of children has become an urgent issue today.

It has been rightly said —

'A child born today in the U.K. stands a ten times greater chance of being admitted to a mental hospital than a university... We are driving mad our children more effectively than we are genuinely educating them.'

❖ Peace in Ancient Indian Society

The Indian's daily life is his or her religion. He or she lives what he or she believes. An Indian is a practical psychologist. Their philosophy of living is honest appreciation; and they are sincerely thankful to God for the common things of life. Their wants are legion and needs are few. They struggle towards perfection. They have no attachment for places or things. While taking bath, they bless the stream and thank God for water. For food they are grateful to God while eating. When gathering herbs for medicine, they are reverent in that the herb sacrifices its life to save them! Among ancient Indians, greatest was shown towards the aged. To them, it is obvious that with their years they must have gained wisdom out of experience. There is no double standard of morality; and they had no poor houses and no orphan asylums. Orphans were adopted by friends of parents and immediately assume equal right with the children of the new household The marriages were usually successful and couple will grow old in harmony with each other and their children. In this regard, let us not forget J. Krishnamurti's words —

"Without an integrated understanding of life, our individual and collective problems will only deepen and extend. The purpose of education is not to produce mere scholars, technicians and job hunters, but integrated men and women who are free of fear; for only between such human beings can there be euduring peace."

Concludingly, it may be said as follows:

An important feature of the Indian man's psychology is that he never acts hastily or through impulse, but only after deep thought and consideration, weighing all sides of a problem. The Indian is not easily fooled. His discrimination is highly developed, for he is fully aware that he must seek guidance from his higher consciousness within himself. He is therefore not easily influenced by outward appearances.

He accepts responsibility with full labour and adversity with great patience; he argues that he must have deserved them or they would not be his.

He masters pain and emotion with self-control, and courageously meets his problems in life. And his problem is greater now than it has ever been.

He knows well that it is not enough merely to believe; he must act.

He incorporates natural, ethical and physical law into his very being, he makes them part of his daily life, the basis of his religion, and the foundation of his home. This is the essence of his whole psychology and his philosophy of living and the very core of his being. It is true Brotherhood.

The Ancient Indian served life through his or her body, served nature through the mind and served God through his or her will.

World War II brought enormous loss of life and cruel suppression of human rights. The extremely painful experience paved the path of peace. In order to prevent the repetition of such painful events, various nations were compelled to sit together to ensure lasting peace in the world. The result was formation of United Nations. This world body announced the Universal Declaration of Human Rights on 10th December 1948. The declaration included thirty human rights; and it was expected that all the nations would take steps to assure these rights to their citizens. But this hope did not materialise soon. This resulted in another World Conference of United Nations. In 1993, in Vienna, a week of intensive debate brought the nations to the decision that the declaration of Human Rights of 1948 should be translated into deeds. Media too gave sharper focus and wide publicity to these human rights. It then became worldwide that promotion of human rights is the first condition for promotion of peace! Human rights is a global phenomenon and it refers to fundamental freedom and basic liberties without which, men, women and children cannot live with respect and dignity. Concept of Human Rights is rooted in freedom of thought and dignity of human being.

Now, the question arose what should be taught through human rights education. As an answer to this question, it may be said that all human rights education should bring awareness among students of schools, colleges and universities regarding all the rights laid down by United Nations. Next step should be to point out that rights and duties are to be taken like two sides of the same coin and therefore one cannot think of rights without duties. Actually, rights are achieved by performing the duties. If we want rights without performing the duties, we will find peace disturbed everywhere and world will enter into the grip of violence and war. If we want nobody to snatch our rights, we also should not snatch anybody's rights. Such a situation of give and take alone can save our rights. This makes us clear to know that our stress should not be on achieving of human rights but on performing our duties connected with those human rights. Rights and duties always go hand in hand.

In ancient India, human rights were achieved through **Dharma** or human duty. Almost all Hindu scriptures preach people about Dharma. Because of this, people never committed any sin. Result was that sin or crime was brought to its lowest level. Even kings were controlled by this tradition. It was an open secret that if one performs his or her duties, (धर्म), the human rights become automatically safe. This is the reason, people in ancient India talked of rights. Hindus were told of only one right and that is performing of one's duties. In Bhagwat Geeta, Lord Krishna clearly says "कर्मण्ये वाधिकारस्ते म फलेषु कदाचना." This means, a human being has just to perform his or her duties and not to think of the results. With this strategy of dharma, Ancient India has achieved the target of safeguarding human rights of its citizens.

As our world becomes a global village, the need for better understanding and communication among people from different countries increases. Many of today's issues transcends local or national interests and action. For example, common markets, resource shortages, ethnic conflicts, nuclear proliferation, natural disasters, drugs and environmental problems cannot be handled by individual nations. Relations among nations require meeting and communicating with people of diverse cultural backgrounds.

Whether the situation is bilateral or multilateral, technical or ideological, or the standard for success, victory or a problem solution, individuals from many countries must interact. Ideally, they come to understand their basic cultural differences and create commonalities in their interaction, which facilitates communication and problem solving. More likely, they assume that they all share the same reality and consequently experience conflict in their interaction until they find that they do not have one reality in common.

Betty Peardon, a noted peace-educator, once said — "the failure to achieve peace is in essence a failure of imagination" [personal communication]. Throughout the history, a considerable amount of human and economic resources have been invested in creating new and deadlier means to wage war. The time has come to invest the energy and resources to innovate and create new and deliver means to wage peace.

Edward Hull hypothesizes that the majority of our cultural categories, plans and rules are unconscious. To understand our cultural frame of reference or mindset [Fisher] in any given situation — that is, how we typically think and feel — requires understanding our unconscious subjective culture and the context of the situation. In the past, when societies were simple, and more homogeneous than today, such an understanding was often based on such familiar ethnographic markers as skin colour, religion, nationality, gender or background. As societies become complex and fluid, the subjective cultures of their members diversify, and these same ethnographic markers are often unreliable guides for predicting and understanding their mindset and also behaviours [*Avruch* and *Black*, 1990, 1991].

We develop and use symbols that give meaning to out social activity, language, our most complete category system is the primary mode of communication in our symbolic environment. Its inherent reciprocity makes it ideal for constructing common meaning. As individuals [parents, children, teachers, students] interact within a symbolic environment, the shared meanings they create and use become beliefs and attitudes in their subjective culture, and norms and values in their common culture or society.

Although mediation become more familiar in recent years, its use is often hindered by ignorance, resistance, and a lack of social support. But, research indicates that mediation is effective in many conflicts; yet, most of the people are reluctant to try it because they are unfamiliar with the process and distrustful of their adversary. For this reason, exercising tactful but firm pressure on antagonists to try mediation is often extremely helpful.

International meetings and negotiations ultimately depend on human perception and behaviour, and that, such perception and behaviour are critically affected by the mindset of every negotiator, mediator and educator. Differences in perception, cognition, reasoning and communication style can lead to misconception and miscommunication that hamper these meetings and create conflict.

Problem solving and decision making are processes interwoven in many cooperative conflict resolution processes. Both training and practice could benefit from approaching the conflict resolution process as one in which diagnosis, development of alternatives, choice and commitment take place; and in which problem solving as well as decision making both play a critical role. Constructively negotiating and resolving conflict with others requires self regulations to strategically modify one's own thoughts and actions so as to allow progress toward important shred goals. An essential ingredient is to cool hot impulses, emotions, and automatic fight-or-flight reactions that are easily triggered by the stress inherent in conflict. Modern India as well as the whole world is facing the problem of protecting human rights of citizens and bringing peace to this planet. But we could not get success. Reason is, we have left the path of Dharma! In fact, all religions teach of human duties and human values. Most of the religions embrace peace and harmony as central tenets. Through the ages, principles such as 'love thy neighbour' and sanctity of human life have been ardently promoted by religion. In spite of this fact, violence continues unabated From Indonesia to Ireland, Middle East to Kashmir, India to Nigeria, Christians, Buddhists, Jews, Hindus, Muslims and Sikhs justify the use of violence on the grounds that they are protecting their identity and interests. This is the reason for conflicts in different parts of the world. Entire human family is divided by religion with several major religious powers locked in perpetual rivalry. Many have argued that religion is, in fact, a force for division rather than unity! Jonathan Swift has rightly said — "We have just enough religion to make us hate, but not enough to make us love one-another." How very true! Further, it has been noted by many historians too that religion is more likely to be a cause of war. Religion has been tightly interlocked with political and military entities. Hence, one should not forget that various religions of the world have caused fierce fighting between followers of different religions. It is because of this fact, Mahatma Gandhi gave us the idea of "'सर्वधर्म समभाव'", which means that we should treat all religions with respect and treat them equal. Because, all the religions teach their followers to follow their human duties, they are helpful in promoting human rights and world-peace. In this light, religion is the best agency to inculcate human values.

Thus, preachings of various religions, respect for all religions, equality of all religions an co-ordination between all religious should also be the part of human rights education. This will create the atmosphere of love among all people irrespective of their caste, colour and moreover we should stress upon those human duties which are connected with various human rights. Then alone human rights education will promote peace in the world.

Concludingly, it may stated that each one of us have got a very limited time. Hence, we should not waste it jut by destroying others' lives by hatred, anger, jealousy, disliking, etc. Let us develop a courage to follow our own intelligence and intuition. Let us work for peace and harmony, and make a world a better place to live in. Let us get rid off religion. The idea that the evils of this world could be greatly minimised by eliminating religion has been loudly accepted in recent years and it is time to realize a Universal Religion!

All the above said things can be achieved when our teaching aims at:

- fostering attitudes of tolerance, respect and solidarity,
- providing knowledge about human rights,
- developing means by which human rights can be translated into social and political reality.

To be cultured is development. Indian concept deems such development synonymous to culture but inclination towards materialism rather than custom is more conspicuous feature of Indian republic. Today, we are developing not in civilization but in aberration, which is resulting in the emanation of copious problems like issues of globalization, global warming, arms dealing, inter-ethnic fighting, racism, sexism, and plethora of other problems, many people are left feeling frustrated, disillusioned, or at the very least, confuse about what they can do to alleviate the violence of these problems and bring some peace and relief to others in need.

Development is important for human welfare and economic progress of the country but the nature of development, which is prevailing and being practcised is utterly not the need of humanity. However, unfortunately entire humanity is running behind such uncanny development, the reason for which lies in ignorance. Therefore, it is very essential, in any form of life, to deepen the quality of awareness. To deepen the awareness, which is born out of true perception and understanding, is one of important quality of any form of education and therefore, to deepen one's awareness is one of the principal teachings of all the forms of education. Learning in its pristine form takes place everywhere, not only within the confines of places called schools. Somewhere along the way, though, the real joy of learning disappears and a dark cloud of academic violence sets in. This is problematic because it forces students to learn by fear rather than by desire, which is making the learning messy and unorganized. To be very precise, I have seen the students so tired from working late, already getting deficit sleep and learning how to function as a working zombie is preventing them to dream big or dream at all. This academically violent system creates a fear of stepping out of line, of being too creative, of making the teacher look stupid or saying something too smart, of conforming to state standards.

How can such common filthy practices of educational system be removed? Can peace-education have any bearing with the situation? What does peace-education have to do with academic violence? It is time now to ponder upon it seriously.

Peace-education, should be an interim movement because it is not the end result — there is no finality in peace-education. Peace-education should be a movement to humanize education, to integrate meaningful learning experiences, foster communication and personal reflection, self-actualization and realization of talents to make the world a better place. Peace-education should treat students as active participants in their learning and challenge them to look at their participation in the world as something connected to their daily learning experience. It should promote an interconnected view of the world and give students tangible skills in conflict resolution and managing everyday problems they encounter. It should also teach students to look at problems in a radical way — radical in the Indian sense of getting to the root.

Nevertheless, it is a big responsibility to take on the task of educating peace. Teaching peace is about having a ready-made soapbox to promote progressive social issues. It is not about pitting progress against conservatives. In addition, it is certainly not about telling students what they should think. Teaching peace is about helping students to find their voices, to listen to themselves and to each other, to trust themselves and to learn more about themselves. Teaching peace is about the process of facilitating a fair and balanced discussion, ensuring that all voices are heard and respected. Teaching peace ultimately is about addressing why our schools, homes, communities and countries are increasingly violent. Why do we live in a world where husbands kill their pregnant wives for dowry, where parents abuse children, where priests are involved in sex scandals and money laundering, where workers shoot up their workplaces, where heart disease and cancer wreck families who sit down to dinner eating genetically modified foods and argue throughout the meal from start to finish — or don't sit down together at all. Do we really have any solution for all this?

Global Peace through Indian philosophy lies in:

1. The factors that influence the viability of peace-education in the world which include the philosophical underpinnings of peace-education, ideological issues concerning the relationship between academia and politics, and the structural and economic conditions in the world. An examination of Gandhi's legacy provides an additional

lens by which to understand the ways in which peace-education has and has not been developed in India.

2. With the basic skill that every man should learn *i.e.*, reading, writing and arithmetic, the fourth should be "reconciliation", which will help man confront his biases and redirect his aggressive behaviour, learn to negotiate and discover non violent means to related to one another.
3. Peace-education more so emphasizes the need to draw out the instinct to live peacefully which resides in each individual as a response to the world they live in. Peace-education is therefore both a philosophy and skill that prepares people, young and old, to negotiate on behalf of themselves and the world in a peaceful manner. It seeks to transform conflict using non-violent tools and bases itself in the values of compassion, interconnectedness, justice and harmony.

Education is a life-long process, hence, one should remember to remain a life long-learner. In the Indian society, philosophy of life-long learning is embedded in the society, culture and education. India has a rich and long tradition of learning through life.

Social economic and technological changes of the post decades are making teaching more crucial than ever. The information and knowledge for society needs a continuous change; and accordingly Information and Communication Technologies [ICTs] have brought new possibilities into the life-long learning.

The role of teacher changed from knowledge transmitter to that of learning facilitator. Hence, challenges of the 21st century for teachers as educational professionals not only to impart knowledge but also to train students will skills to become better and competent learners. As a result of such ICT based education, students can translate bookish knowledge to real life situations. Therefore, keeping futuristic view in mind, it is very important to prepare future teachers with the knowledge and skills of using ICT.

Information and Communication Technologies [ICTs] is thus a key for unlocking new possibilities to envision modern education. Hence, future learning is now focussing on learning beyond the classroom and curriculum. Institutions of learning, particularly higher learning needs to upgrade their teachers by offering retraining programmes.

❖ Indian Philosophy: Champion For World Peace

In fact, the most important achievement of India thought is Indian philosophy. The Indian philosophy of humanism reflects that the religious thoughts have put forward the simple preposition that the chief end of human life is to work for the happiness of humans upon this earth and within the confines of Nature.

In ancient India, philosophy always held a predominant position and spiritual motive dominated the life. People in India is the ultimate relation between the truth of philosophy and the daily life of people that makes it always alive and real. The philosophy of India's oldest religion, Hinduism has taught the world both tolerance and universal acceptance. The greatest aspect of this religion is that it accepts all other religions as true and respects them. India, as a nation, sheltered the persecuted and refugees of all religions and all nations on the earth which came to her. It has also forgiven and sweetly mingled with its invaders the Muslims and the Christians. Indian culture is dressed with profound understanding of human nature and their relations with each other. Each of the existing religions in India taught the ultimate lesson of truth, non-violence and universal brotherhood that forms the base of Indian Philosophy King Ashoka substituted religious propaganda for military aggression as his instrument for unifying the world. Gandhiji lead us successfully through the struggle for political liberation. Though Gandhiji made it impossible for the British people to go on ruling India, at the same time he made it possible for them to withdraw without irretrievable discredit and disgrace. Gandhiji inspired the people to keep the struggle on a spiritual plane that was above the level of sheer politics.

Gandhiji's theory of non violence has been put into practice for many years by India, whether it is in its relation with its neighbouring countries, dealing with terrorism or even internal strife. If India were ever to fail to live up to this Indian heritage, it would be a poor lookout to mankind as a whole. This is the great spiritual responsibility rests on India.

If one analyses violence in a family or in an office or in a school or in a nation, the violence may be from one person with power who might not have understood the other or may be the irritation which entered the heart. The killings of religious saints and great statesmen, innocent people by terrorists are condemnable irrespective of their identities or the religion to which they belong.

Here Gandhiji's tool of truth and non violence found in his movement of satyagraha is more than a political tool of resistance. It helped us to move towards a holistic approach based on truth and moral courage. The similarity of the satyagraha to some of the greatest philosophical and religious tenets of India has been noted and has now merged to be called the Indian philosophy. Gandhiji said, "My life is my message." His life is replete with examples of how he was able to diffuse very tense and violent situations through listening, talking, empathizing, fasting, being willing to suffer and other non-violent interventions. Gandhiji's analysis of means and ends may also help in attaining peace. Peach-education should emphasise not only on ends but lay more emphasis on means. This completely coincides with our religious law of "karma". If end achieved is moral but means immoral or violent, then the end is unjustified. Spirituality, serenity, peace of mind are the ultimate yearnings of the human mind. These can be achieved through the postulates of Indian philosophy — "Dharma" and "Karma", two foundations of the Indian philosophy.

Indian philosophy has inculcated the culture of peace and non violence for the children of the world. So, let us build a culture of peace around. Let us with empathy, help one another stand against and eliminate poverty, prejudice, discrimination, war, hatred and violence. Let us adopt the "Satyagaha" as a way of life. On personal front — satyagraha involves life committed to truth and hard work. On political front — satyagraha involves using non-violent means to curb opponent and convert him not coerce him to submission.

Many a time, a question is asked — 'Is Religion A Force For Peace?' It is indeed difficult to give a correct answer to such a question. Most religions embrace peace as central tenets. Through the ages, principles such as love of neighbour and sanctity of human life have been ardently promoted by religion. Yet violence continues unabated. In a review of recent conflicts in the different parts of the world, the book entitled 'Violence In God's Name' says — "from Indonesia to Ireland, Middle East to Kashmir, India to Nigeria, the Balkans to Sri Lanka, Christians, Buddhists, Hindus, Jews, Muslims and Sikhs justify the use of violence on the grounds that they are projecting their identity and interests. In fact, many argue that religion is a force for division rather than unity. A Muslim scholar, Mohsen Hojjat, acknowledged that disunity along Muslims is the root cause of problems in Islamic World! Furthermore, it has been noted by historians that religion is more likely to be a cause of war.

To this day, religion has been tightly interlocked with political and military entities. It can be said now that, let the world become a better place to get of religion. The harsh reality is that while the 21st century has been heralded as a time for peace, today we are in a world thriving in a culture of violence. The tragedy is that many of the frontline persons involved in these conflicts are young people, who have played into the hands of terrorists, rebels, dictatorships, and greedy militia. How do you make transition from a culture of violence to a culture of peace? The issue therefore is how to address the threats of violence and how to start building a culture of peace.

In fact, religion is conspicuous and an indispensable factor to the evolution of the state. Religion and Kinship move hand in hand in cultivating respect for authority, loyalty and obedience. The strong bonds of blood-relationship and Kinship are consolidated by equally. Strong ties of common religion and worship. In any religious field, authority is always yielded by priests.

All over the world, impact of religion on the life of the people has been great in all ages. In the evolution of the state, religion played a very important part in strengthening the ties of oneness in families, clans, tribes and kingdoms.

THE TRUTH IN ALL RELIGIONS

There is truth in all religions. Almost all people on this planet have found a right path because of religion. All religions stem from the same source. Just what that source is, no one is fully sure, yet, true to say that we all are a part of that sources. We are one; one human family, one world, one universe. As the Dalai Lama says it:

> *"All human beings come from a mother's womb. We are all the same part of one human family. We should have a clear realization of the oneness of all humanity."*
>
> *"All religions are essentially the same in their goal of developing a good human heart so that we may become better human beings."*

Usually, people try to define themselves with labels, but labels are mere words. One need not care if he or she is a Buddhist, a Muslim, a Christian, a Hindu, a Jew, a follower of many paths, or any other faiths, traditions, that are spread throughout this world. One just has to know that 'we are all one.'

In every religion, there is a lot about love; and there are many, many similarities in all the religions of the world, one just has to take a special notice as to where the wording of 'The Golden Rule' actually comes from. In fact, all religions have such 'rules'. The religions are in Bold Print, followed by the quote and then the source text.

An Ancient Precept

Baha'i

'Blessed is he who preferreth his brother before himself.'

Baha'Ullah, Tablets of Baha'ullah, 71

Buddhism

'Hurt not others in ways that you yourself would find hurtful.'

Udana-Varga, 5: 18

Christianity

'All things whatsoever ye would that men should do to you, do ye even so to them.'

Jesus, Matthew 7:12

Confucianism

'Do unto other what you would have them do unto you.'

Analects 15: 23

Hinduism

'This is the sum of duty: do naught unto others which would cause you pain if done to you.

Mahabharata 5: 1517

Islam

'No one of you is a believer until he desires for his brother that which he desires for himself.'

SUNNAH

Jainism

'In happiness and suffering, in joy and grief, we should regard all creatures as we regard our own self.'

Lord Mahavira, 24th Tirthankara

Judaism

'What is hateful to you, do not to your fellowman. That is the law: all the rest is commentary.'

Talmud, Shabbat 31a

Native American

'Respect for all life is the foundation.'

The Great Law of Peace

Sikhism

'Don't create enmity with anyone as God is within everyone.'

Guru Arjan Devji 259, Guru Granth Sahib

Zoroastrianism

'The nature only is good when it shall not do unto another whatever is not good for its own self.'

Dadistan-Dinik, 94:5

Thus, there is truth in all religions; and that truth comes from the same source. There are many paths to divine.

"Do not say, 'I follow the one true path of the Spirit,' but rater, 'I have found the Spirit walking on my path.' For the Spirit walks on all paths."

Conclusion

In a world where many religions suffer from increasing tensions, conflicts and violence, making peace a tangible reality is of critical importance.

The world today, is, indeed in search of new culture and a common system of values and new behavioural patterns for individuals, groups and nations; because, without them, the major problems of international and internal peace cannot be solved. What we achieve spiritually inwardly will change outer reality. We do not need a magic to change the world; we carry all the power we need inside ourselves already. It is the greater awareness and knowledge of oneself ultimately helps develop a more grounded belief in oneself courage, determination and above all, humanity. The concept of Vasudeva Kutumbakam are extended to include the world as one's family. Such a view promotes fellow beings.

♣♣♣

3

CONFLICT ANALYSIS

Very rightly it has been said by Helen Keller that "The best and most beautiful things in the world cannot be seen or even touched. They must be felt within the heart."

Now, for the above said fact by Helen Keller, the following things are required —

1. We must try to discipline our mind.
2. We should try to have a disciplined physical behaviour.
3. Also, there must be discipline in our speech.
4. So too, increased awareness in our actions is a must.
5. Then, we should not forget about contented living. Now, as far as the core values are concerned, the following four are very important —
   (*i*) Resolution of inner conflict —
   (*ii*) Self-Knowledge
   (*iii*) Spiritual needs
   (*iv*) Meditation.

The statement in the preamble of the UNESCO's Constitution, "Since war begins in the minds of men, it is in the minds of men that the defences of peace must be created" provides a guiding principle for the above said things. Learning to be means to learn to live peacefully with oneself. Peace can be experienced within ourselves. Inner peace arises out of intrinsic inner richness such as compassion, spiritual joy and wisdom. Here, one must try to understand the significance of beingness. It is that state of mind where a person experiences the joy of wholesome living. This means, there is no conflict. What is a conflict, then? Conflict is a situation between two parties over a disagreement on an issue it which they have a common interest.

An exploration of the elements of peace includes examining the language we use in our daily discussions. Tolerance, understanding, empathy, cooperation and respect for differences in others are at the core of our peaceful experience on earth, but each of us may interpret these concepts somewhat differently based on our cultural values, our life experiences, and our belies about the world. It is important for all of us to share an understanding of these concepts as we talk about our attitudes and values and as we describe and analyze situations for elements of peace or conflict. Most people agree that conflict is a negative force that we should try to resolve in order to achieve more positive states, such as, harmony, understanding and peace in our lives. Nevertheless, conflict exists at all levels of social interaction from personal inner conflict to global war and international violence. We cannot avoid conflict, but we can definitely find way to deal with it that will reduce its impact on our lives and every exploit positive effects related to conflict situations. For example, conflict resolution techniques provide us with ways to examine a situation and our responses to the situation that allow for more peaceful living.

Clarifying the elements with a situation that are sources of conflict is an important first step in resolving the conflict. Conflicts of resources, conflicts of needs and conflicts of values are the most common categories of conflicts, and it is often difficult to label the conflict precisely. Since resources, needs and values are interrelated. Conflict resolution experts have identified many skills that facilitate the smooth management of conflict. These include working cooperatively, developing good communication skills, learning to express our feelings constructively and increase of diversity. Basic procedures setting out the processes of conflict resolution are —

- **Analysis:** Defining the conflict.
- **Ideation:** Developing alternative solutions.
- **Strategy:** Gaining a working knowledge of conflict resolution techniques.
- **Risk-taking:** Choosing to act on solutions.

The following list is a selection of the most common pro-social behaviours and communication skills that have been identified by peace educators for classroom instruction and practice. The first two entries are themes in previous chapters of the Peace-education volume.

Speaking for a purpose: We understand that the perceptions of others may be different from our own and that what is said should serve a mutual productive purpose, such as clarification of the situation. Conflict resolution skills are important for clarifying situations.

Listening attentively and reflectively: Listening to others in order to understand the whole message (the emotions, perceptions, and context as well as what was said) is an important stage in effective communication. Reflection of the whole message back to the speaker communicates that he or she has been understood.

Promoting self-esteem, dignity for oneself, and respect for the feelings and rights of others: Use the language of acknowledging, labeling, and affirming pro-social behaviour (*e.g.*, generosity, being considerate, helpfulness) in the classroom in your interactions with students. Also, encourage students to use pro-social behaviours in the classroom. A basic starting point is to provide language activities that show students the functions of thanking, apologizing, welcoming, and other pro-social norms of behaviour. This can be done through dialogues, role-plays, modeling, and other activities.

Speaking about yourself instead of about the other person: It is more effective to describe an issue in terms of its impact on you rather than in terms of what the other side did or why you think they did it. Practice the use of "I" statements instead of "you" statements to clarify facts and feelings in practice situations, skits, and dialogues.

Speaking with positive emotional expression: Sometimes when we are angry or highly involved in discussing an issue, we say things that do not promote effective communication. Speaking clearly and firmly so that the other person understands — but without negative emotion — involves making statements without blaming, name-calling, raising one's voice, or demanding. It means avoiding "put-downs" and the use of "loaded" negative language. We can help students to be more aware of negative emotional language and its effects on communication by analyzing scripts for instances of its use. Discussing alternative language that would clarify and improve the understanding of the listener will help learners to be more sensitive in choosing what they say and how they say it. After analyzing and discussing the scripts, students can write and act out both positive and negative versions of dialogues that contain emotional expressions, paying attention to the non-verbal as well as verbal expressions they choose to use.

Understanding possible barriers to effective communication and how to diffuse them: Possible barriers to communication are the behaviours of interrupting, dominating the discussion, criticizing, judging, teasing, and using emotional language. Learners need to be able to analyze the discourse of conversations in order to identify these communication "pitfalls". Further instruction on alternate behaviours for similar situations will help learners to communicate more effectively.

Empathy requires that we extend ourselves beyond the level of cultural and sociological understanding and try to make connections on the level of individual personality. Our own moods, feelings, emotions, and attitudes change constantly, and it is even more challenging to predict the emotional state, needs, and reactions of others from a different culture. Practicing empathy is a psychologically and emotionally demanding interpersonal skill, but one that is necessary for effective cross-cultural communication.

Reasons for educating for peace in the language classroom are:

- To make learners aware of the basis of conflict and how to resolve conflict in their daily lives.
- To prepare students to become good citizens of their communities, nations, and the world with skills to promote peace and human dignity on all levels of interaction;
- To use the classroom as a microcosm of a just world order, in which the global values of positive interdependence, social justice, and participation in decision-making processes are learned and practiced.

How to do it? Implementing peace-education in the language classroom can be achieved several ways.

- Using topics that raise the issues related to peace and cultural understanding in our classrooms, language teachers can give students basic information to help them develop positive attitudes and values related to "peaceful" living".
    - Engaging in activities that encourage cooperation, consensus building, and reflective listening gives students the skills they need to meet and resolve conflicts.

Confronting issues and problems related to the topics will provide opportunities for students to develop problem-solving skills and critical thinking skills along with language skills to express themselves clearly and convincingly.

An exploration of the elements of peace includes examining the language we use in our discussions. Tolerance, understanding, empathy, cooperation and respect for differences in others are at the core of our peaceful coexistence on earth, but each of us may interpret these concepts somewhat differently based on our cultural values, our life experiences, and our beliefs about the world. It is important for us to share an understanding of these concepts as we talk about our attitudes and values and as we describe and analyze situations for elements of peace or conflict. Most people agree that conflict is a negative force that we should try resolve in order to achieve more positive states, such as harmony, understanding, and peace, in our lives. Nevertheless, conflict exists at all levels of social interaction, from personal inner conflict to global wars and international violence. We cannot avoid conflict, but we can find ways to deal with it that will reduce impact on our lives and even exploit positive effects related to conflict situations. For example, conflict resolution techniques provide us with ways to examine a situation and our responses to the situation that allow for more peaceful living.

Clarifying the elements within a situation that are sources of conflict is an important first step in resolving the conflict. Conflicts of resources, conflicts of needs, and conflicts of values or goals are the most common categories of conflicts, and it is often difficult to label the conflict precisely since resources, needs, and values are inter-related. Conflict resolution experts have identified many skills that facilitate the smooth management of conflict. These include working cooperatively, developing good communication skills, learning to express our feelings constructively, and tolerance of diversity. Basic procedures setting out the process of conflict resolution are:

❖ Tolerance and respect for Dignity and Identity

Peace-education means promoting the development of the learner through an emphasis on understanding individual rights and responsibilities. This understanding is critical as we strive to build a culture of peace. However, before we can truely understand notions of citizenship and participation (ourselves in relation to others), we have to first ask the question, 'who can I?' Identify is what distinguishes us from others and joins us to them. Our unique identities and common human dignity provide the foundation for peace-education.

❖ Social Justice and Civic Responsibility

A fundamental aspect of educating for peace is to make learning come alive. Peace is not something 'out there' to be objectively studied and understood; rather, its seeds are sown in every relationship in all learning communities around the globe.

Social justice is the principles of positive peace that complements the notion of peace as the absence of direct and institutional violence (negative peace).

❖ Leadership and Global Responsibility

In the new millennium, as the world becomes increasingly interdependent, students face even greater challenges and opportunities. Peace-educators seek to harness the energy and intellect of youth in the hope of building a sustainable culture of peace together. Worldwide, educators, activists and all members of the international community are emphasising the need to challenge the decisive aspect of increased globalisation.

Pupils must be put at the centre of everything we do. No calling is more noble, and no responsibility greater, than that of enabling men, women and children, in cities and villages around the world, to make their lives better. Only when that begins to happen, will we know that globalisation is indeed becoming inclusive, allowing everyone to share its opportunities.

Students are becoming subjects in the world; and building leadership and a sense of citizenship in the world enables students to participate and make their voices heard.

Everyday we hear of conflicts between and within communities. Children are exposed to these conflicts through television and conversation within adults. Some are also exposed to violence in other forms, closer to their everyday lives — domestic violence, child labour, social inequities. We need to talk about these in class, dissect and explore them and their relationship to our lives, so that we can show children that there are other ways to resolve problems. It is important that as educators, we have to use whatever opportunities we have to reinforce values of cooperation and peaceful existence.

It is important to note that children look beyond physical or verbal retaliation as a means of solving disputes, and see why peace is an imperative, not just a desirable goal. Unless such issues are brought to the fore and discussed there is a danger that children may not be sensitized to the consequences of violence on any scale.

❖ Peace as Resolution of Inner Conflict

In fact, peace can be experienced within ourselves. According to Sigmund Freud, our mind is just like a battlefield where the life instinct is in conflict with the death instinct. It is at the superficial level of mind, inner peace can be experienced through resolution of psychological conflict. Most of the conflicts are internal, *i.e.,* within ourselves. The nature of inner conflict has been described by various psychologists. For instance, Curt Lewin has shown that we have three basic types of inner conflicts. They are:

1. Approach-approach conflict.
2. Avoidance-avoidance conflict and
3. Approach-avoidance conflict.

1. Approach-approach Conflict

In this type of conflict, a person is caught in between two equally attractive objectives out of which he or she can select only one. The correct example would be the choice between two equally attractive jobs.

2. Avoidance-avoidance conflict

Here the person tries to avoid two equally undesirable objectives where he is forced by circumstances to select one rather than selecting the other. For instance, when a person is offered with two jobs and both are equally unattractive. However, he is forced to select one.

3. Approach-avoidance Conflict

In this type of conflict, there is such a situation when a person is both attracted as well as not attracted by the same objective. He definitely wants something for a certain reason and at the same time, he does not want it for some other reason.

Erick Erickson has once said that the man's psychological growth results from the healthy resolution of inner conflict. This means, in each growth stage, man is confronted with a basic psychological conflict. But sometimes, at certain circumstances, the inability to resolve this inner conflict block his or her future growth and further, this leads to pervasive behaviour. In fact, this has been proved by the experiments conducted on many criminals and terrorists; and some of them had been led to adopt violent ways of life as a result of inability to resolve their inner conflicts. [*e.g.*, deep hurts experienced during childhood]. It is a fact to note that when a person who is unable to live with himself in peace, cannot live in peace with others. Now the question that jumps like a boomrang is — "How can we help our youngsters to resolve their inner conflicts?" "What can be done?" Answers to such questions may be given by saying that resolving of an inner conflict may be done through —

(*i*) gaining self knowledge,

(*ii*) knowing pupils' spiritual needs,

(*iii*) adopting meditation as a classroom practice,

(*iv*) finding imagination of children, and

(*v*) by practising awareness.

(i) Gaining Self-knowledge

For resolving one's inner problems, one must try to learn to look within and observe how the mind works. Here, one has to perceive the problems distressing the mind and understand clearly. The more one tries to understand himself or herself, means he or she is more matured enough psychologically. Thus helping children to look within and understand the self is an important life skill. In fact, much disruptive behaviour of people is because of their unresolved deep inner conflict. Historically, in various parts of the world, peace-education has been referred to as Education for Conflict-Resolution, Life-skill Education, Education for Liberation and Empowerment, Disarmament and Development Education, etc.

(ii) Knowing Pupils' Spiritual Needs

Peace-education deals with the depth of human mind; and peace in one's self arises from deep human spirit that underlies all faiths. Spirituality means the essence rooted in man, which seeks for the fulfillment through expressing and experiencing goodness in the highest degree. It drives us for the search for true meaning and values lying deep within us.

The needs of children are not many; but they are definitely strong and delicate. Children want to experience joy as well as wonder and then feel good too. Such as children's spiritual needs; and depriving them of such needs means withholding their blooming personalities!

(iii) Allowing Meditation as a Classroom Practice

It is a fact that we all know that when a mind calms down we have a feeling of joy and peace which to unfold within us; and one of the effective way of realizing peace within is meditation. Meditation is taught in all religions. But by meditation we do not mean a particular practice adopted by a particular religion; but by meditation we mean an open mental activity. It has been proved by various studies that meditation improves creativity. When the mind settles down in concentration, an intense sense of peace begins to unravel. In fact, all meditations are exercises in developing calmness in the mind. Meditation leads to effective learning because of the awakened sense of enthusiasm and liveliness.

Stephanic Herzog after conducting the experiment on meditation in her classroom practice, says —

> *"Meditation is a technique in getting in touch with our own inner wisdom. Most children grow up without ever discovering that there is a source of wisdom and strength and love inside themselves. They look to their parents for these qualities but often parents are lacking in these qualities in themselves."*

She further reported —

> *"After using meditation in classes, I began to notice a definite change in the students' ability to be self-disciplined and self-motivating. I do not think that children in my classes were conscious that they were gaining these qualities ... It all happened just naturally."*

❖ Types of Meditations for Children

- Take the class out to an open air or a quiet place. Let them sit quietly and listen to the sounds in the environment. This helps to develop awareness towards the surroundings.
- Making children sit quietly and to repeat in mind "I am a peaceful soul." Watching a tree with a silent mind.
- Sitting quietly and concentrating on breathing in and out.
- Looking at a flower and concentrating the mind on it.
- Imagining a beautiful natural scene.
- Imagining a trip in a strange land or garden.
- Sitting quietly and experiencing the feeling of a noble human quality, such as kindness, and joy. Apart from experiencing inner calm and beauty of imagination, meditation opens the door to understanding one's own thought process. It is this self-knowledge that brings emotional maturity in us. As educators we have to find effective methods of helping children to understand themselves better.

❖ INTENDED BEHAVIOUR

❖ Discipline in Mind

- Control of emotion enjoying being calm
- Tolerance
- Self-management

❖ Discipline in Physical Behaviour

- Correct body postures
- Calm manners

(iv) Finding imagination in Children

It is a fact to note that children are gifted with high imaginative power. However, as they start growing up, most of them lose this important capacity.

Creativity spurts out from imagination. However, unfortunately, these children's imagination power, are curbed by the teachers or other adults at home [not always — but it does happen!]. Children's imaginations are neglected and no opportunity for the development is provided. But, those who try to curb the imagination of the children, fail to notice the fact that when children's imaginations are suppressed, it may find other ways or moods of expression such as day dreaming, self-enclosure, anti-social behaviour, etc. Hence, teachers have to help their children to build positive self-images by encouraging, providing opportunities to express themselves.

(v) Practising Awareness

An act of establishing awareness is possible only through meditation. Being aware means being alert, being attentive, being mindful, etc. It is basically a survival life skill. For example, take an example of the function of awareness in an act of crossing a very busy street. A moments lost of it may take away one's life. Thus, awareness is a basic function of intelligence. Hence, it is essential that children have to be trained in being aware of dangers in their surroundings. Be it home, school, playground or road. Awareness brings self-control as well as sharpening of attention. Awareness develop one's sensitiveness towards the body. There is also what is called as subtle level of awareness. Say, for instance, when I say I am angry, I know that I am angry; and when I am confused, I do know that I am confused. This is what is known as subtle level of awareness. In fact, we are inclined to be carried away by our own desire, anger and illusion, and most of our inner conflicts arise out of the lack of self-understanding.

❖ Core Values and Attitudes for Eliminating Conflicts in Children

Human values are internalized sets of belief or principles of behaviour held by individuals or groups. The values which follow are chosen because they are deemed to be universally acceptable and desirable, based on what is best described as "International Humanism" and are embodied in such characters as the Universal Declaration of Human Rights, The Rights Of The Child, Women's Rights, etc. Consistent with such values and attitudes that should be nurtured in the learning process and which themselves strongly influence the process, quality and outcomes of both learning and assessment are —

(I) Core Values and Attitudes for enhancing Peace-education —

1. Values and Attitudes Related to Human Rights and Democracy.

2. Values and Attitudes Related to Cooperation and Solidarity.
3. Values and Attitudes Related to Preservation of Cultures.
4. Values and Attitudes Related to Self and others.
5. Values and Attitudes Related to Internationalism.
6. Values and Attitudes Related to the Protection of the Environment.
7. Values and Attitudes related to Spirituality.

(I) Core values and attitudes for enhancing Education for Peace

1. Human Rights and Democracy.
2. Cooperation and Solidarity.
3. Preservation of cultures.
4. Self and others.
5. Internationalism.
6. Protection of the Environment.
7. Spirituality.

1. Values and attitudes related to Human Rights and Democracy

- Dignity.
- Equality.
- Justice.
- Protection of the Rights of all peoples.
- Participation.
- Freedom of speech and expression.
- Freedom of belief.

2. Values and attitudes related to Cooperation and Solidarity

- Love of peace and harmony.
- Interdependence.
- Conflict resolution by peaceful means.
- Mutual understanding, co-operation and respect among individuals and societies.
- Culture of peace and co-operation.

3. Values and attitudes related to the preservation of cultures
    - Respect for the family and all of its members.
    - Appreciation of one's own culture.
    - Appreciation of the world's cultural heritage and human achievement.
    - Sensitivity to social and cultural change.
4. Values and attitudes related to self and others
    - Self awareness, reliance, self-esteem and discipline.
    - Respect and empathy in our relationship with others, loving and caring.
    - Moral courage.
    - Open-mindedness, truthfulness, tolerance, equanimity and reconciliation.
    - Inquiry and creativity.
5. Values and attitudes related to Internationalism
    - Awareness of the rights and duties of citizenship.
    - Equality among nations.
    - Harmony between nationalism, regionalism and internationalism.
    - Awareness of global issues and their peaceful resolution.
6. Values and attitudes related to the protection of the Environment
    - Interdependence of people and nature.
    - Appreciation and commitment to maintain and improve the environment for the survival of all species.
    - Promotion of a sustainable environment.
7. Values and attitudes related to spirituality
    - Aspiring to inner-peace.
    - Freedom of thought, conscience and belief.
    - Freedom of religious practice.
    - Mutual respect for the religious observance of others.
    - Equality of treatment of religion by the state.

(II) Skills

The skills that the students needs to develop to be proactive and peacemaker are as follows —

1. Thinking Skills:

Critical Thinking: The ability to distinguish fact, opinion and belief; to recognize bias and prejudice; to identify issues and problems as well as the assumptions in an argument; to reason correctly.

Information Handling: To be able to form a hypothesis and test it; to know where to look for answers and how to select and reject information.

Creative Thinking: To seek novel solutions and answers; to think laterally and approach problems from multiple perspectives.

Dialectical Thinking: Thinking about more than one point of view; understanding both points of view; being able to construct an argument from either point of view based on knowledge of the other.

2. Communication Skills:

Presentation: To be able to clearly and coherently explain ideas.

Active Listening: To listen carefully, understand and acknowledge the views of others.

Negotiation: To recognize the role and limitations of compromise as a tool for the cessation of conflict; to carry on a productive dialogue towards the resolution of a dispute.

Non-verbal Communication: Recognizing the meaning and significance of body language.

3. Personal Skills:

Co-operation: To work effectively with others towards a common goal

Adaptability: Willing to change opinions in the light of evidence and reason.

Self-discipline: Ability to conduct one's self appropriately and manage time effectively.

Responsibility: Ability to complete tasks in an appropriate manner.

Respect: Listening sensitively to others; making decisions based on fairness and equality; recognizing that others' beliefs, views and ideas may differ from one's own.

Thematic Areas

The intention of outlining thematic areas is to provide teachers with ideas for exploring some key issues in Education for Peace. Issues chosen to illustrate these themes should reflect the principle of *"think globally, act locally."* The teacher as a role model is undoubtedly a *key player* in the living expression of peace-education; the *"peace classroom"* is a model to which we should all aspire

❖ Summary of the Thematic Areas

1. Human Rights.
2. Social Justice.
3. Development,
4. Population concerns,
5. Health and Habitat,
6. Cultural Diversity,
7. The environment

1. Human Rights — Topics to be included

Personal rights	Rights in relationships between people:	Public freedom and political rights
– right to live in freedom & safety	– family rights	– freedom of expression
– anti-slavery	– children's rights	– freedom association
– protection under the law	– minority rights	– democratic rights
– right to citizenship	– property rights	– freedom movement
		– religious freedom

2. Social Justice — Topics to be included

– provision for social welfare	– affirmative action policies	– unemployment
– equal access to education	– poverty	– work

3. Development — Topics to be included

- inequalities in wealth and income distribution between nations and within nations
- the impact of individual choices on the production and consumption of goods
- alleviating poverty

- the role of international agencies and agreements
- the role of multi-national corporation
- the responsibilities of developed nations
- trade and development
- appropriate technology
- measures of economic development

4. Population Concerns — Topics to be included

- growth demographic
- migration
- effect of natural disasters
- refugee issue-structural
- urbanization

5. Health and Habitat — Topics to be included

- adequate living space
- homelessness

III. Staff Development in Education for Peace

Staff development is an integral part of this process. Teachers should receive formal training in education for peace. The whole climate of personal and professional relationships within a school must be in keeping with the goals of international understanding, democracy and peace. Any of the following models and instruments may be useful for addressing staff development needs.

- Schools may choose to allocate at least one staff meeting per year to review the school's response to Education for Peace.
- Staff members might be identified to co-ordinate Education for Peace activities.
- Team teaching will be effective in generating a collaborative approach.

Year level meetings can be used to generate ideas, co-ordinate activities, and expose teachers to the themes of Peace-education. The purpose of these meetings could be expanded to:

- Define Peace-education aims, strategies and goals for the grade.
- Raise the level of awareness amongst teachers about Peace-education.
- Monitor progress.

In teaching style, teachers in schools developing an Education for Peace program seek to fully incorporate basic procedural values, such as open-mindedness, fairness, and respect for truth and respect for reasoning. Open-minded inquiry flourishes best in a peaceful learning .environment A tolerant, warm, supportive, caring, learning environment is just as important as the question of content.

❖ CASTE CONFLICT

Caste was a very serious issue of Indian society for more than ten centuries which was not addressed by the leaders of the society till 19th Century. This had very serious impact on the growth and development of India in the fields of Education, Agriculture, Industry, Knowledge, Economics, Politics and almost all other fields and pushed India into the category of 'Undeveloped Country' which can be better called as 'Backward Country'.

Dr. Ambedkar worked as a sociologist towards the wider/larger goal of 'reconstruction of the social order' of the Indian society which was majorly a Hindu society and was based on inequality between castes. He realized that social reforms would not be sufficient and the standards and values put forward before the society by religious scriptures required to be replaced by the values and standards of liberty, equality and fraternity. And this demanded the reconstruction of the Social order.

Amount of tension and conflict in the society is increasing each passing day and is thus affecting the lives of so many.

Children are affected psychophysically by the violent surroundings. Hence it has become more important to care for their well-being and then try to eliminate fears and anxieties that are generated within them.

Concludingly, it may be said then that the success of educational system depends largely on quality of teachers. Hence, the role of teachers cannot be ignored at any cost as the destiny of the nation is being shaped in our classrooms [*Kothari Commission,* 1964] by the teachers.

Education, in true sense of the team means freedom from narrow feelings and sentiments as well as freedom to explore other cultures.

Today there is an explosion of knowledge due to advancement in the field of science and technology. These advances have ultimately resulted into making a successful trip even to the moon!

Our old ideas are gradually changing giving place to new ones, values and traditions. New knowledge is discovered in different subjects. However, side by side such an ever-developing store of our knowledge has created certain problems and questions too! The world population growth has brought forth a tremendous knowledge for the ideal education for all; and even more so, the provision of opportunities for life-long learning. It is estimated that nearly one third [1/3] of children who start the first grade will drop out before completing grade time.

Social terrorism has really become a complicated problem of today. It has become an obstacle in the way of progress. Terrorism as defined in the sense of fear, created by some immoral deeds is really a curse today! So too, violence in educational institutions has acquired a global dimension bringing with it enormous problems for guardians, teachers and also administrators in all places. Stress has become the one biggest component in today's myriad life-problems. Whether it is a case of a frustrated employee, depressed student, a house-wife, a desperate teacher or a highly furious administrator, all have one thing in common and that is stress! Stress is the contribution of our fast-pace in life; everybody trying to reach the moon instantly. A German philospher Humboldt has said — "No man's life is free from struggle and stress, but each one may build up his or her own happiness by making himself or herself independent of outward conditions."

Because of the above said facts, it is felt that Conventional Methodologies in teaching and student-counseling have to give rise to new turn — Personality Modification. Teacher preparation need to give more thinking, teacher's role needs to meet new challenges.

♣♣♣

4

BRINGING ABOUT CHANGE BY PEACEFUL MEANS

Peace-education programme in schools is basically a character-building intervention based on a human, civic, moral, and spiritual value-system with stress on developing peaceful living competencies in children. In fact, each and every good school has moral and value educational programmes in some form or another and, a good peace-education programme can incorporate all such good efforts. What is needed is the fact that the innovation should be evolutionary. A teacher has to take lot of care while designing a peace-education programme for his or her class. However, if it is to go beyond the classroom level interest, support of the principal as well as the management is very much essential. But before that, it is very much necessary to find out the strategies and techniques of non-violence. For this, the identification of the existing needs is the first thing to be taken into consideration. Very often, we find, a sort of constant restlessness in students. This state of mind is witnessed in the form of quarreling, fighting, complaining, shouting and many other disturbing forms of violent behaviour. Further, the students are also seen increasingly getting into seeing violent films and also getting involved in many types of gambling. They also seem to take a proud out of masculinity, a fashion that they have learnt from mass media! Hence, many a time, the teachers seem to be not satisfied with the present attitudes and the mindset of adolescent students in the school. For instance, they have very little respect for others, including teachers! The relationship with teachers gets distanced gradually. Mutual respect too gets deteriorated even among themselves. Teachers very often get complaints about bullying. Students attitudes towards country and culture and social problems too, is seen in their non-violent behaviour. Their attitude becomes purely negativistic. Teachers wonder how they could overturn such students into good citizens and want to change the way things go.

Thus, it may be stated firmly that every school has violence in it, and it grows in subtle forms. Violent behaviour in schools is seen in the following five different forms —

1. Verbal Violence : Insulting, name-calling, threatening, cursing, shouting, alluding, labelling and arguing.
2. Psychological Violence: Blaming, ridiculing, condemning, scorning, embarassing, revenging, anonymous writing.
3. Physical Violence : Slapping, caning, kneeling down, torturing, assaulting hitting, pulling ears or pulling hair.
4. Criminal Violence : Stabbing, shooting, destroying property, raping, child abusing, vandalizing, gang assault.
5. Structural violence : Pushing students to compete with others, comparing individuals, keeping children sitting passively for hours, neglecting students' special needs, harsh imposition of rules, externally imposed discipline, drilling.

Obviously, the actors of the above said violence are the members of the staff and students except on rare occasions where public intruders break in and commit aggressive acts.

❖ Teachers' Violent Behaviour

In certain schools, the tradition of physical and verbal violence still continues by way of caning, scolding and other ways, in spite of all the propagation of child rights going outside. They are justified in the name of education.

When a teacher commits an act of violence against children say, caning or harsh abuse, the happy social climate of the whole school is affected adversely. A negative climate, charged with fear and threat emerges. Constant teacher violence implies the following negative impressions about the school.

(*a*) Distanced teacher-pupil relationship.

(*b*) Deteriorating teacher professionalism.

(*c*) Inefficiency of school management to control such unprofessional behaviour.

(*d*) Teachers' lack of skills in maintaining a positive discipline.

(*e*) Children's apathy against the present quality of education they receive.

What is the way of discouraging teacher violence in school? The following guides may be helpful.

1. Conduct school-based staff development session on:

   Maintaining positive discipline in school

   Methods of motivating students.

   Method of classroom management.

2. Conduct programmes to improve teacher-pupil relations, *e.g.*,

   Drama

   Education trips and hikes

   Staff development in innovative teaching methods.

3. Discourage the use of caning and other forms of physical punishment.

4. Adopt humanistic and democratic strategies in the maintenance of school discipline.

❖ Students Violent Behaviour

Violence or aggression is generally defined as acts committed with the intention of hurting, injuring or harming another person.

Words or thoughts that express the intention of hurting are also a part of aggression.

However, all forms of children's aggressive behaviour need not to be taken seriously. Naming some forms of behaviour as violent may not be fair. For instance, children fight for fun and to test their strength. Such behaviours are not malignant, vicious and therefore not aggressive. Such behaviours seem to play a part in children's psychological development. They disappear naturally with the other stages of growth. Parents and teachers should be concerned only when such behaviours seem to establish as a pattern of personality by repeated acts.

Media is undoubtedly the greatest medium of communication in our society. The crucial matter is how does media's portrayal of violence affect us? Mass-media is any of the means of communication as television, newspaper, reaching large number of people.

Violent behaviour describes more serious forms of physical aggression that pose significant risk of serious injury to victims in order to exploit and subjugate. There is close relationship between aggressive behaviour and exposure to media. Major work in this context is done by social learning theorists which hypothesized that media characters serve as models of aggressive behaviour. The child does not necessarily adopt the behavior portrayed but the media images provide a model as standard for what may be considered normal and acceptable.

With the advent of mass-media including television and more recently video, computer games, children are largely exposed to aggressive images. Violence among children and youth is increasing to a great extent making it plausible to study the link between the two, even though we believe that the primary causes for aggressive behaviour in children are to be found in their family environment, social and economic conditions in which they are raised.

Children have always learned how to behave in the world in form of stories of their times and the mass-media are todays story tellers. If the stories our children see routinely involve violence as the solution to problems their personal values and cultural world view will have a complete different dimensions. Parents and teachers indeed have got an important role to play. Several scholars have pointed out that as media content has increased in violence in past few decades. Media continues to have a rising influence over the youth. These influences include media in the form of television, music videos, computer games, Bollywood glamour etc. The effect of these exposures are both psychological and physical. The exposure to violence in media increases aggression in children in form of bullying, disrespect, rude language. It also brings in desensitization in them. This also causes increased blood pressure, heart beats, and respiratory problems. Excess exposure causes psychological trauma like anxiety and depression.

There are many steps each one of us can take to reduce the amount and impact of violent images in our lives and lives of our children. This would help to bring up a widespread social change. Lets break the circle of blame and start building a movement for caring culture.

Despite the fact that violence is experienced by individuals (in varied forms and varied situations) it primarily has social and societal context. Thus social context impacted by the ideologies caste, class and gender produce violence. Moreover the ideologies of caste class and gender impact the social structure and institutions, making these agents of violence. Hence violence encountered by the social groups marginalized and subordinated by the ideologies of caste, class and gender confront social institutions, social structures as agents and sites of violence. In other words, institutions, structures as well as members of dominant and ruling castes/ classes (which dominate these structures and institutions) are sources of violence against the marginalized sections of society.

❖ Violence Against Women

Though verbal, physical, direct, indirect types of violence have existed in the world for centuries, today this grim facet of human life poses a serious threat as never before. Women are specially vulnerable to violence in domestic, occupational and social spheres. Violence against women is the most pervasive yet least recognized human rights abuse in the world.

Violence against women takes various forms like the killing of female fetuses and newborns, and sexual violence. Due to their peculiar socialization, many women perceive themselves as inferior, defenseless and weak. The predominance of the 'soft-gentle' traits and the relative lack of the 'strong-tough' traits in women's personality, their financial and emotional dependence on others, their stereotypical and regressive portrayal in mass media, and the traditional social conditioning of men and women are some of the important factors that need to change if the increasingly disturbing problem of violence against women has to be effectively dealt with.

There has been limited identification of the problem of battered wives and their long-term effects have been very much a recognized as well as a most concerned fact today. It is a serious problem, no doubt. Most of the cases of attempted suicide, show that these woman suffer from "deliberate self-harm", "adjustment disorder" "anxiety" and "depression."

❖ Violence At Workplace

India ranks 128 among 149 countries in the Global Peace Index prepared by the Institute for Economics and Peace in consultation with an international panel of peace experts from peace institute and think-tanks. The study ranked these countries from 2007 to 2010, and India's rank in violence is going down in these four years, the lowest being 107 in 2007. This is a very dismal record of India in the context of extent of violence.

Violence is the expression of physical force against one or more people. Worldwide, violence is used as a tool of manipulation and also is an area of concern for law and police which make attempts to control it. Violence takes place in different sections and sectors of society such as family, social organizations, political and religious fields, industrial organizations etc. Violence in industrial organizations may be called as violence at work place. The noticeable instances of violence at work place are found since the inception of the industrial revolution in 1760. At the workplace, the causes of violence are inter-group, inter-community, inter-caste, inter-religion, and inter-union rivalry. Sometimes it takes very ugly form causing the loss of human lives and destruction of properly.

❖ Form of Aggression

Psychologically we can classify aggression in to live basic forms of expression.

1. *Organized group aggression:* where a gang perform an aggressive act, with a pre-planned course of action.
2. *Direct aggression:* where people directly express physically or verbally their anger against others.
3. Indirect aggression is mostly manipulative where a person pretends to be nice, but works behind towards the destruction of others.
4. *Symbolic aggression:* conveys the message of violence through a symbolic action. They are mostly used in political and public campaigns.

5. *Instrumental aggression*: is used as a strategy or a means to achieving a certain goal.

❖ Ways of reducing Students' Violent Behaviour

1. Prepare a school policy for prevention of violence in school.
2. Based on the policy, draws a violence control programme as a part of discipline management.
3. Build school as a community, based on the principles of mutual respect and co-operation. Emphasize the value of non-violence as a part of the school tradition.
4. Make learning meaningful and joyful. Improve the quality of education in the school to the satisfaction of the students.
5. Implement a fáir system of discipline control using positive techniques.
6. Encourage each class to draw a code of conduct and maintain it.
7. Refer students found in vicious aggressive behaviour to counselling.
8. Keep the school under surveillance during intervals, especially in those areas where bullying and other anti disciplinary behaviours could occur.
9. Implement school timetable effectively so that students find no time to engage in anti disciplinary activities.
10. Organize a surveillance system to check students' movements after school is over, *e.g.*, on their way home up to a certain limit.
11. Implement the school timetable tightly allowing no free periods, during special seasons when ragging and bullying increase in the school. (*e.g.*, beginning of the year/ when new students enter high school.)

Concludingly, it may said that many a time most of the disciplinary problems reflect the inefficiency of the school. What is really necessary is to correct the causes of conflict. It should not be forgotten that peace-education is basically a positive approach to school discipline. Hence, what is required is to find out ways by which some good schools maintain their discipline by discussing with their principals. So too, discussion with the colleagues is a must.

But, one may question — 'Why at all there exist a non-violent behaviour?' The reply to such a question is — 'Non-violent behaviour takes place on account of conflicting situations!' Hence, it now becomes essential to know everything regarding conflicts.

In fact, conflict is everywhere, because it is a part of life! Conflict arises because of individual differences and diversification of the society.

❖ Definition

Many a time a question is asked — 'What is the exact definition of a "conflict?" And, as an answer to this question, it may be said that a conflict is —

- — a difference of opines,
- — a clash of wants,
- — a situation that arises from a disagreement between two persons,
- — a broken relationship
- — a vicious competition against one another.

Inability to resolve conflict at the beginning, leads to complication and intensification. In the process of escalation of conflict, our friend, colleague or neighbour with whom we have the disagreement, turns gradually to be our rival, opponent, and finally the enemy. The initial open and friendly situation that was there, at the beginning, becomes gradually tense and hostile.

❖ Causes

Why do people get into conflicts? It is because of the other person's way of behaviour. When two or more people are at conflict their interests may be concerned with,

- — commodities at stake, *e.g.*, object, land, money.
- — opportunities at stake, *e.g.*, opportunity for gain, privileges.
- — principles and values at stake, *e.g.*, religious beliefs, ideologies, cultural values.
- — territory at stake, *e.g.*, house, land, physical space, road, status
- — relationship at stake, *e.g.*, trust, promise, personality clashes.

Conflicts become destructive simply because of the lack of skills in handling them. If they are handled properly towards positive results, it will bring growth, and renewed relationship, sense of fun and self-confidence. Recall a conflict you have resolved constructively. Destructive conflict occurs when the value of the conflict is not understood and when you react with negative emotions to it.

In a constructive approach to conflict resolution, we —

1. Control our negative emotions.
2. Listen actively.
3. Speak efficiently.
4. Deal with the other, as a person with a problem, need and human reaction.
5. Face the issue directly and precisely.
6. Separate the problem from the person and adopt a problem-solving approach.
7. Show understanding and be understood.
8. Be willing to change your position in face of facts and reason.
9. Use a sense of humour.
10. Generate alternatives acceptable to both you and the other person.
11. Speak to the point.
12. Use interpersonal skills.
13. Be persistent.

Our general tendency when confronted with a conflict is an attempt to win by defeating the other. This pushes the other person too to adopt the same approach. As a consequence, distinctive competition emerges out of the situation. Hence, in a conflict, a solution is to be reached through understanding the following three basic stages —

1. Confrontation,
2. Negotiation, and
3. Implementation.

In fact, children's world has number of conflicts. It means, they are not free from conflicts. Hence, a teacher needs to know the nature and types of conflicts that children have. In helping them to learn conflict resolution the teacher can take examples and cases from their conflicts.

❖ Conflicts at Homes

- Jealousies among the brothers and sisters, by comparing with each other on what they get from parents.
- Problems of equal treatment, privileges and personal rights.
- Problems arising from carrying out their responsibilities.
- Inability to deal with parents' anger, negative comments and violence.
- Deprivation of freedom to play, meet friends and express oneself.
- Deprivation of parents' love.
- Deprivation of physiological needs, *e.g.*, food, proper shelter, owing to low income.
- Problems with elder brothers or bigger kids in the neighbourhood.
- Drunkenness of father disturbing peace at home.
- Instance of child abuse, *e.g.*, severe punishment.
- Separation of parents.
- False accusations.

❖ Conflict in School

- Name calling
- Being snubbed/being teased.
- False accusations.
- Fear of being unprepared, e.g. not having a pencil, not ready with homework, not having read the lesson.
- Misunderstanding by teachers.
- Negative remarks by teachers.
- Being cheated by a peer.
- Being deprived of opportunity to participation in activities that the child likes.
- Inability to buy things that the school requests.
- Physiological problems, *e.g.*, hunger, low energy,
- Exclusion by peers.
- Adolescent growth problems.

The classroom should have open sessions where children can freely discuss and express their conflicts and problems. Unfortunately the traditional school is too busy to take into consideration this lively aspect of children's growth.

❖ Classroom Practices — Resolving Conflicts Non-violently

1. Find opportunities during the lessons in subjects like literature, history and social studies, to discuss concepts and methods of conflict resolution. Some events in the text provide good case studies for identifying the needs and fears of the conflicting parties, how they failed to reach agreement, their short-sightedness, and the ways they could have found a solution.
2. Appoint one or several classroom mediator/s or peace maker/s in order to help students to resolve their conflicts. This will give them an opportunity to practise conflicts resolution in actual situations. (See School Practices)
3. Organize special sessions/workshops for students on developing skills in active listening, concept analysis, negotiation and problem-solving.
4. Whenever you find vicious conflicts in students, get them to meet you, and do counselling in privacy helping them to understand each others' feelings, explore into their own consciousness to discover the deep cause for such behaviour and their inner unresolved problems. Get them to discuss and resolve their problems, by speaking out, listening to each other, proposing alternatives and finally agree upon a situation.

❖ Hints to Peace Culture-building in school

1. Provide an opportunity for children to discuss their problems openly in the class.
2. Conduct staff development sessions on ways of improving relationships with the teaching staff and students.
3. Conduct session for parents, to draw their attention to children's problems.

❖ Learning Activities

Ask the students only to discuss the basic nature of conflict. Here the curriculum will be social studies [history or literature]. Then, ask them to find synonyms for conflict [*e.g.*, quarrel, fight].

The students may also be asked to write down on a piece of paper the immediate feelings, reactions, memory or thoughts that come to his or her mind when they hear the word 'conflict'. [Expected response anger, assault, violent behaviour, harsh words, etc.]

Next, ask the children to give the definition of 'conflict' and then let it be read out to the class. After getting the definition from them, find a comprehensive definition and then write it on the board. [*e.g.*, "Conflict is a situation between two parties over a disagreement on an issue in which they have a common interest."]

Divide the class in five groups. Give them five minutes to select a type of conflict and rehearse role-playing it. Each group must present their role-play to the class; and every presentation is to be followed by discussions with a view to understand the nature of conflict. In the discussion, the guiding questions will as shown below —

1. What did you learn about the conflict?
2. What are the basic types of conflict?
3. Why do people have conflicts?

Thereafter, the teacher has to build a summary of the discussion on the board.

There is also one more step in the method of resolving a conflict and that is a "dialogue" method. This included in role-play.

❖ Definition and Explanation

A dialogue is a conversation between two or more people. It is also a literary form in which two or more parties engage in a discussion. In fact, dialogue is used as a form of communication used for the purpose of entertainment and instruction. Ultimately, this form has scarcely been modified since the days of its birth. In the East, the genre dates back to the Sumerian dialogues as well as Rigvedic dialogue hymns and the Indian epic Mahabharata.

In the West, however, the literary historians commonly suppose that Plato introduced the systematic use of dialogue as an independent literary form. The Platonic dialogue had its foundations in the mine. But afterwards, Plato simplified the form and reduced it to pure argumentative conversation. Following Plato, the dialogue became one major literary genre in Latin and Greek literature.

Celebrated Brazilian educationist Paulo Freire, introduced dialogue as a type of classroom pedagogy. Freire held that dialogued communication allowed students and teachers to learn from one another in an environment characterised by respect and equality. Dialogued pedagogy was not only about deepening understanding, but, it was also about making positive changes in the world to make it a letter place to live. Today, dialogue is used in classrooms, community centres, corporations, federal agencies and other settings to enable people, usually in small groups, to share their perspectives and experiences about difficult issues. It is used to help people resolve longstanding of contentious issues.

Dialogue is not about judging, weighing or making decisions but about understanding and learning. Dialogue dispels stereotypes, builds trust, and enables people to be open to perspectives that are very different from their own. Since more than two decades, a rapidly growing movement for dialogue has been developing. Dialogue in classrooms started teaching of Social Studies and also educating children with special needs.

In the dialogue class, the students were made to sit in groups; and the already introduced topic was then divided into different portions as issues. Teacher worked as a supervisor. After fifteen minutes, one student from each group presented the conclusions to the whole class and teacher worked as interlocutor. Ending was done with teacher's comments.

What is the feedback? One may ask — Answer is as follows —

1. Students enjoy the activity.
2. A new understanding is there for the already lectured topic.
3. This activity is more than bookish knowledge.
4. Pupils get encouragement for self-study.
5. This method is time-saving and lastly,
6. Dialogue method builds confidence in the learner.

Example: Let us now take the case of handling controlling an anger. In fact, this is an activity about discovering the very many ways of controlling anger. Let us take one illustration. Present the following case to the students. Ram waiting in a long queue at the bus stop. Bus was late and Ram was getting impatient. Ram saw one person getting into the queue. This was really unfair and Ram got annoyed. Ram demanded that this person should go out of the queue. But the person refused saying "I will not go there at the end of the queue. Do whatever you want!" Ram could not control his anger and he assaulted the person in a fit of anger! At last a policeman came and took both of them is police station! Finally, both had to apologise each other! Ram was advised by the policeman to refrain from assaulting people.

Teacher now asked the students the following question —

'What made Ram assault the person?' Teacher asks one of the students to come forward and speak as Ram to explain what went in his mind. And the dialogue continues.

Students are also asked to work in groups and make a list of instructions about ways of controlling anger. They present the methods. Do a follow up discussion with each presentation. Include the following methods of anger control if they are missing.

Do not act or take decisions under the impulse of anger. Postpone action.

Know and accept yourself, that you are angry.

If you happen to explode in anger, be silent, show that you feel sorry and apologise.

In a conflict never react to the other person's words or deeds in anger.

Instead of being harsh, speak to the person, assertively, *e.g.*, "When you speak like that I feel hurt."

If your angry feelings are boiling inside after the incident, release them physically through acts such as swimming, kicking a ball or working hard in the garden.

Teacher then lets the students go in groups and propose a list of instructions on the right way of dealing with an angry person. The children finally give the following guidelines to deal with angry people.

❖ A Guide to Deal with Angry People

Be assertive and avoid being submissive or aggressive.

Listen to the person empathetically, showing your understanding.

Do not react.

Show your understanding using such expressions, as "I can understand your anger here."

Show acceptance whenever you can agree with some of his points, *e.g.*, "There I am with you. There you are right."

If you were wrong accept it, *e.g.*, "Yes. I do accept it."

If you are right, then tell him stating gently, "Look so far I listened to you, now would you listen to what I have to say?"

Try to bring the other person to a problem-solving discussion. [This other person acts as a mediator]

❖ Constructive Conflict Resolution

When we want to introduce peaceful ways of conflict resolution among students, we should know that though conflict is unpleasant, it can be resolved constructive and end happily. Conflict should be identified in its early stages because it is easy to resolve conflict at the very beginning. Conflict needs to be handled well so that it does not turn out to be destructive. When people behave destructively in conflict, they —

(*i*) blame the other,

(*ii*) threaten the other,

(*iii*) challenge the other,

(*iv*) destroy other's property and

(*v*) show impulsive behaviour.

Conflict always ends by turning the other into an enemy and by resentment. When people resolve conflicts constructively, they come out with mutual satisfaction and renewed relationship and with an improvement in self-confidence.

CONFLICT RESOLUTION

Destructive Approach	***Constructive Approach***
1. Emotional Behaviour	1. Mature Behaviour
2. Anger	2. Patience
3. Aggression	3. Assertion
4. Short-sighted	4. Long-sighted
5. Blunting the person	5. Separating the person from the problem
6. Threatening	6. Inviting discussion
7. Demanding the fixed solution	7. Searching for alternative solution.
8. Not listening	8. Active listening
9. Egocentric	9. Problem-centred
10. Non-negotiable	10. Negotiable

❖ Mediation

Let us now try to understand about meditation process.

The main curriculum concern is to give information to the students about mediation.

1. When two parties in a conflict, which they find difficult to resolve by themselves, a third person can intervene between them and help to settle disrupter. This process is called mediation.
2. Mediation is stepping in between two conflicting parties to help resolve their problem.
3. The mediator should be an impartial person acceptable to both parties.
4. You can be a mediator when your friends are in conflict, and when they need someone to step in.
    1. Introduce yourself as a mediator.
    2. Listen to both the parties.
    3. Get them to discuss their problem and suggest solutions.
    4. Help them to select the most agreeable solution and settle the conflict.

Let us have a closer look at the steps:

Step 1: Introducing yourself as a mediator.

Ask the parties, whether they like you to help them to come to a settlement. Take them to a quiet place.

Step 2: Listening to both the parties.

Ask party A to explain what has happened. Party B should listen, without interruption.

Secondly, ask party B to explain what has happened. Party A should listen without interruption.

You ask them more questions, get the matter clarified, to other parties and you as well.

Step 3: Get them to discuss.

Ask them to discuss how to resolve their problem.

Let each party suggest alternative solutions.

Encourage them to explore good solutions.

Step 4: Help them to select the most agreeable solution.

They have to come out with suggestions until they find the most agreeable one. Once they find the agreeable solution, help them to plan the implementation of the agreed solution. How not to restart it after the settlement. What they should do and shouldn't do with regard to the problem.

Congratulate both parties for their co-operation given to mediation. Precept the following case study to the class.

Prem and Janak are studying in the same class. Prem complains Janak is nicknaming him. It is really hurting him. Prem has requested him several times to stop it. But he didn't care. This prompted Prem also to retaliate by nicknaming Janak. As a consequence, they had a heated argument and eventually they started fighting. The resentment is continuing.

Invite three students to come to the front and role-play the three characters. Prem Janak and a mediator.

Check the dialogues that they have written and then as a facilitator guide them through the four steps of mediation described above.

❖ Discussion: Guide Questions

1. What is mediation? Explain it in your own words.
2. Why should a mediator be impartial?
3. What are the difficult situations, a mediator can face in helping to settle conflicts?
4. What are the skills necessary to mediate conflict?
5. "A mediator is only a helper. He does not force his solution on the parties. The parties in conflict should come out with the solution." Comment on the statement.

❖ Negotiation

A conflict never gets resolved unless the parties come to a common definition of their problem. That means, they must agree to what the exact problem is. For instance, in a conflict with someone, I say one thing and the other says another thing as to what the conflict is. Then, it is never solved. This situation is obvious in any outgoing conflict. Here enters 'negotiation' now. Hence, let us see what it means.

Negotiation is a process of reaching a common and fair agreement on a solution of the problem, affecting two or more parties. In negotiating, one asks questions for getting to know the problem from the other's side and trying to explain his or her side. Having thus established the understanding, both the parties try to find a win-win solution. In negotiating, one just asks questions to steer the negotiation on the right track. One may seek specific clarifications on the issues and the other needs of the other party. Active listening is an important skill in negotiation. Active listening involves in giving one's full attention to what the other person is saying, feeding back, encouraging deeper probing, supporting the other person's attempt to find solutions, and then, summarising what has been said.

Over and above what has been said so for, both the parties of a conflict situation should try to find out alternative solutions extensively to the problem. One must not get fixed to his or her position demanding the only way one wants to solve the conflict. Taking the alternative solutions one by one the parties can evaluate them eliminating the unaccetpable ones to them. The evaluation of alternatives goes until they come to one alternative most agreeable to both. In evaluating the implementation, one must try to find out how it works in practice and how people feel about the solution. Perhaps, the parties may need some adjustments as the implementation takes place and the original problem might change. However, if the parties are not satisfied as things go, then, they can resist negotiation.

A life is given to us by God. Life is a very precious thing in the world, but what have we done? We have distorted it to pieces, divided it, brought about violence, destruction, hatred. This has made us all to lead a life that is without love, without compassion, without passion. The greatest man is he who chooses the right with invincible resolution; who resists the temptations from within and without; who bears the heaviest burden cheerfully; who is calmest in storms and most fearless under menace and frown; and who reliance on truth, on virtue and on God, is most unfaltering. And it is peace-education alone that helps for the advancement of human development through learning. Peace-education is fundamentally dynamic, interdisciplinary and multicultural, and it grows out of the work of educators like John Dewey, Maria Montessori, Paulo Freire, Juhan Galtung, and many others.

Building on principles and practices that have evolved over time, responding to different historical circumstances, peace-education aims to cultivate the knowledge, skills, and attitudes needed to achieve and sustain a global culture of peace. Understanding and transforming violence is central.

Peace is understood not only as the absence of traditional forms of direct violence, but also as a positive presence. Educating for and about all aspects of peace constitutes peace-education.

In the classroom, peace-education aims to develop skills, attitudes, and knowledge with co-operative and participatory learning methods and an environment of tolerance, care, and respect. Through dialogue and exploration, teachers and students engage in a journey of shared learning. Students are nurtured and empowered to take responsibility for their own growth and achievement while teachers care for the well-being of all students. The practice of peace-education is an opportunity to promote the total welfare of students, advocate for their just and equitable treatment of youth, and promote individual and social responsibility for both educators and learners. Through pedagogy and social action, peace educators that there are alternatives to violence.

'Peace is possible for life at all stages and it is up to man to choose his destiny or to suffer from the horrors of war. Today mankind is at the cross-road where he has to choose with courage, determination and imagination.' **— Federico Mayor**

Peace this moment in our history is only a dream that is far from the actual daily reality of the majority of the world's population and the rest of God's creation on earth. Conflicts, violence and wars are on the rise globally and there is a remarkable increase of structural violence within and among nations. The present global situation makes it even difficult to imagine what a peaceful world and earth look like, or how within the present political, economic and military global frameworks we could even begin to imagine a peaceful world.

India is a multicultural, multi-ethnic, and multi-religious nation and has to learn to live with it to its best advantage. Harmonious living together in Indian society, as well as in every nation, has its foundation on the informal, non-formal, and formal education of all the children and youth living here, and this is the great responsibility of teachers and school administrators as well as parents, families, and the community. In the language of UNESCO, War begins in the minds of men'. Therefore, the remedy also has to take shape in the human minds. So there is a great need to train human minds to work towards peace. It is high time to review our curriculum and give a place for Peace-education in our curriculum.

Centred on developing the capacities of learners, peace-education is relevant in a variety of different educational settings from rural to urban, school-based to community, and within formal curricula or non-formal popular education projects. To a large extent, the social, cultural, economic, and political contexts in which educators work shape the specific content and methods they choose. However, the central knowledge, skills, and attitudes discussed in the Content and Methods section are relevant across educational environments. Many teachers infuse peace-education into traditional academic subjects such as literature, math, science, history, language, civics, and the arts. Various aspects of peace-education may even serve to enhance learning across subjects, as indicated in a recent conflict resolution initiative in the United States. Ultimately, educating for peace is as varied as the teachers who practice it.

On the basis of the above said things, it becomes essential to design a peace-education programme for schools. Hence, let us now discuss about this.

❖ Classroom Practices

By effective characterisation of the core value of positive perception, the teachers will be able to bring out positive changes in students. For this, it is essential to determine the intended behaviour in the students.

> Children generally absorb living qualities such as positive outlook from social learning. In this regard, teachers as role models are very effective. When a teacher has genuine good qualities in herself, her ways of responding to daily situations and life-style exhibit them. Children tend to admire and internalize them.
>
> Life stories of great men and women inspire us with the power of positive thinking. The school's texts can encourage children's character building by including inspiring deeds of positive qualities such as courage, determination, persistence and creative problem-solving. However when they are lacking in the texts, the teacher can supplement them. She can also encourage children to read such biographies.

Appreciating students in a way that brings out their best is an art, teachers can really learn and practise. A general guide is given below.

Learn as a teacher to express yourself in positive terms even in the most difficult situations. For example, instead of remarking 'You are weak' say, 'I am sure you can catch up with this subject easily.' Another example: A student does ten sums and brings the exercise book for you to mark. You will find that all the sums are wrong. Here instead of saying 'Very poor', you can comment 'Your effort is admired'.

Encourage students' efforts using such phrases like: 'You can', 'You have the capacity', 'I am sure you will be able to do that'.

Inquire when appreciating group assignments, 'How did you do it? Who did these? What difficulties did you have and how did you overcome them?'

Instead of denouncing a student for his problem behaviour, show a model student and appreciate him or her. Try to maintain discipline in the classroom through positive evaluation.

Instead of saying generally 'Good' for a student's work, say a drawing, appreciate the features specifically, *e.g.*, 'You have selected your colours to suit the scene. Specially the clouds over the setting sun are beautiful'. Such comments help students to improve their creativity and techniques.

Certain hints, the teachers should care given below:

1. Have a series of short speeches in the morning school assembly to introduce positive thinking and values related to it.
2. Organize a series of lectures to introduce lives of great characters, *e.g.*, Mahatma Gandhi or Abraham Lincoln. In these, talks stress how they faced the challenges of life positively.
3. Develop self-evaluation instruments for students to help their character-building.
4. Invite model persons, like national level scholars, poets, artists, writers, and scientists to school and let students listen to them.

5. Organize displays and exhibitions of students' creative work at the levels of classroom, section, school and community to help them get recognition.
6. Identify creative strategies to provide positive evaluation to students.
7. Organize student personality skill development training sessions in such areas like leadership, human relations, communication and creative thinking.

The things that a teacher should do are as follows:

(*i*) Conduct a peace-education need identification survey in the school and then present it to the staff.

(*ii*) Study good peace practices in other schools.

(*iii*) Draw up a programme for the school.

To assure oneself, it is necessary on the part of the teacher to check the preparation, counsel, facilitate and supervise the implementation. It is very much essential to check what has happened and to what extent things have gone according to the plan.

Last is evaluation, *i.e.,* to judge the worth of a programme.

❖ Cooperative Designing

This is an activity about cooperation.

Level: Primary as well as secondary.

Curriculum Concern: To develop creative imagination in children.

Objective: Learning to work in groups.

Materials: A large paper for each group to draw and pastels.

❖ Activity

Class is divided into 5 groups. They are asked to design a small town with all the facilities. The group then decides what kind of town they should design. They draw it cooperatively. On completion, the group presents their design to the whole class.

A co-operative relationship also helps to create a positive social climate in that it discourages individualistic an self-centred behaviour in the classroom. Mutual appreciation helps to elicit the best in students. Organizing such events as birthday celebrations, get-together parties, singing, short excursions and other socializing activities are also effective in climate-building.

Outcome is as follows:

It reduces restlessness of the students in the classroom as well as in school.

It implements strategies to prevent student conflict.

It develops awareness project for students.

It identifies preventive strategies that could be taken to stop conflict behaviour.

Let us now peep through few curricular subjects in the light of peace-education and jot out ways of presenting them in the classroom.

❖ Language

Language as a subject offers exciting possibilities of using a variety of creative activities in learning it. Integrating such activities makes learning language alive as well as interesting. Among the creative activities are:

(*i*) Role play

(*ii*) Instant drama

(*iii*) Simulation

(*iv*) Imagination trips

(*v*) Creative writing *e.g.*, writing letters to imaginary people.

(*vi*) Co-operative story-making.

(*vii*) Writing books *e.g.*, my family, my life story, etc.

Such activities increase participation and brings in the affective domain in learning. Appreciation and enjoyment of literature helps the emotional development of children. The capabilities of the language as a subject can be extensively explored in inculcating peace-values in children.

❖ History

History is nothing but a story of man's process through time. This can be presented either through a narrow or broad perspective. A narrow perspective presents the events in isolation and single track often biased ethically, religiously or nationally. On the contrary, the broad perspective presents the events in relation to social, political, economic and ideological forces and the background prevailing during the particular period concerned.

The right approach to teaching history can build peace through the opportunities it provides to understand and appreciate other cultures, religions and to realize the strengths as well as weaknesses of man. It helps us to understand the nature of the oppressions, exploitations, invasions and destructions committed by our ancestors against humanity. For instance, how destructive a war can be and how power can blind men. Reading history, which is mostly the story of man's greed and aggression provides insights into the natural human psyche and the need to change it in order to ensure the survival and advancement of mankind. It turns our attention inward to see how the old psyche is still in operation with its roots in the primitive and medieval mentality seeking for security in ethnic centredness, religious fundamentalism, power craziness, selfishness, and aggression.

Unfortunately even in many school textbooks, history is presented from a single side. Take for example, how Hitler and his Nazi campaign are presented. The writers have been unconsciously led to present Hitler as a hero. History is not only the story of war. It is also the story of peace. But very little attention has been given to portray the peace side of the history. To illustrate the point, let us again go back to Hitler's Nazi campaigning. He massacred nearly 6 million Jews systematically in his mania to preserve the pure German race. A child may wonder during the history lesson what the civilized world did to stop it. And consequently, he may learn that the civilized way to respond to oppression and violence is to be passively silent about it. This wrong learning takes place, due to the negligence of giving the peace side of the story. In fact, the civilized world protested against the massacre of Jews. Some people in other countries worked dedicatedly to create pressure to stop it, in their own ways. There were even Germans who attempted at protesting.

Some Jews in the concentration camps bravely stood in their moral strength and died honourably as heroes at the hands of the Nazi, soldiers. But the history writers grossly neglect that side of the story. They also do not tell us about the feelings of the oppressed people.

History, as a subject can also be used to practice non-violence related to various core values such as positive perception, empathy, alternative vision, critical thinking and responsible decision-making. Using such methods as role-plays, group discussions, drawing and debates makes learning history lively and interesting.

In fact, through history one can understand where we are now and where should we go from here!

❖ Religious Education

It is a matter of concern to know whether this subject has been taken up in a regular curriculum. However, it is a fact to note that religion as a subject in the school curriculum can distinctively contribute to peace building!

If at all, teaching of religious education is concerned, then, it must be a child-centred approach. The teacher should encourage religious enquiry, discussion and adopt experience base, in place of teaching domination lecturing, advocacy and patronizing methods. The teacher should use creative methods to develop friendly, tolerant and respectful attitude towards all religions. The teacher should discuss in depth human issues such as purpose of living, nature of suffering, death and ignorance. In such a discussion, the teacher can bring in the perspective of world faith and thereby help in broadening children's vision.

The teacher can also make use of meditation constantly to awaken spirituality.

❖ Mathematics

Mathematics in traditional curricula is presented in an isolated subject; but this can be related to peace-education in very many ways. Mathematics can be used for more concrete activities, assignments and exercises related to reality in order to raise awareness on national and global issues affecting mankind. For instance, at the secondary level, mathematics can include calculations of percentages and ratio of population growth, infant mortality, adult literacy, unemployment, life expectancy, etc. Teachers can design many meaningful exercises based on figures in population growth, education, health and economic development.

Mathematics also provides an opportunity for cultural understanding through studying different mathematical systems in the world and the contributions made in different cultures. Basics in astronomical mathematics can provide insights into the ways the universe operates.

❖ Social Studies

The purpose of social studies is to broaden the children's vision of human society in order to qualify them to be good citizens.

The importance of social studies lies on the ground it forms to discuss issues affecting the globe. Many important themes like democracy, citizenship, human rights, child rights, social justice and problems of underdevelopment could be discussed on that ground. Students come to know major current issues of their society and of the world, such as international conflicts, environmental problems, and advancements of science through it. Various projects can be designed under this subject related to peace building.

Examples:

1. Weekly presentation of global news in morning assembly.
2. Publishing a handwritten or printed magazine/wall paper on current issues related to the subject.
3. Visiting historical/archaeological/geographical sites.
4. Organizing exhibitions on world heritage and other important themes.
5. Conduct community surveys/studies on themes related to developmental issues.
6. Organizing school and public seminars/lectures/discussions on current social issues.
7. Organizing campaigns to raise awareness on issues affecting the people and environment.
8. Viewing video and film shows on related issues.

❖ Science Education

Science is pure knowledge that has nothing to do with human or social issues. It has little or no relation with other subjects.

Science is the only true knowledge. It is fixed and therefore no one can do anything about it.

In fact, science is concerned with the needs and interests of mankind and human welfare. Scientific knowledge is ever evolving and everybody interested can participate and contribute to the advancement of science.

Here it is worthy of mentioning what the physicist Victor Weisskopf said about scientific thinking. He observed:

"Human existence depends upon compassion, and curiosity leading to knowledge, but curiosity and knowledge without compassion is inhuman, and compassion without curiosity and knowledge is ineffectual."

In conclusion, it may be said, then, that these methods such as cooperative learning etc. can improve the quality of teaching and learning process in the classrooms. Hence, it is essential to set a period at least once a week in the class to voice and express students' problems related to learning and other needs with the teacher. Therefore, taking prompt action into address children's problems and needs is very much needed. When the teacher feels that students are beginning to show restless behaviour, the teacher has to start relaxation exercises, meditation or short energizing physical games.

Perhaps a teacher from a good school may not see such deficiencies and tends to think that peace-education is only for problem -schools but not for his school. In fact, starting from problems may not appeal to some. Instead one can start from a positive approach and identify the necessary developments in children from the existing situation. Strengthening the present positive attitudes and behaviour is always necessary. Perhaps when the positive qualities develop the negative ones may easily disappear. Even a best school needs to keep going all the good traditions established therein. Introducing new traditions and attitudes are necessary all the time. A school has to continuously work to strengthen and nourish the existing school culture.

❖ Ways of promoting Peace through the hidden curriculum:

- Clean and attractive buildings and grounds.
- Flexible seating.
- Multicultural environment through activities like celebration of festivals.
- Using democratic decision making.
- Encouraging team-work and group exercises.
- Avoiding verbal, physical and psychological violence in the classroom.
- Evaluating according to the development of each student with his past performance and not with respect to each other.
- Keeping the school open for the use of the community.
- Letting parents and the community, communicate with the school administrators and staff.

In conclusion, let it be said that schools should be the vehicles of positive change, prejudice. Verbal violence and physical violence should not a part of its structure. Schools should reflect what society believes to be good rather than what is undesirable.

Peace-education does not teach students what to think, but rather how to think critically. Peace-education aims not to produce but to transform. It consists of people "consciously striving to educate their successors not for the existing state of affairs but so as to make possible a future better humanity." [John Dewey, *'Democracy and Education'*].

One way to meet the challenges of peace-education is to build bridges of support among key participants. Just as learning takes place in a broader social context and not exclusively in schools or classrooms, so peace-education relies on families, communities, and social networks to affect positive and lasting change. The notion "think globally, act locally" is central to educating for a culture of peace in that it links theory with practice, international issues to individual efforts. As a peace educator, you need not work alone. The international peace-education community is active and growing through networks, publications, global campaigns, national initiatives, and international programs. Concerned citizens, educators and activists of all ages around the world are promoting and building peace through education.

PERSONALITIES AND ROLE MODELS

❖ Mahatma Gandhi

"There is no way to peace; peace is the only way" said Gandhiji. How very love!

Martin Luther King used to say that Mahatma Gandhi was probably the first person in the history to lift the love ethic of Jesus above mere interaction between individuals to a powerful and effective social force on a larger scale. Gandhi preached and practiced that love that suffered was more powerful than the force that inflicted pain and suffering. For him, non-violent insistence on truth was in fact a "moral equivalent of war". Those who are genuinely creative are the people who enjoy some mental health and face personal, inter-personal and other kinds of problems with poise and equanimity. They are not cunning but are altruist. Using Gandhi's words, we can say that the freedom of the sky is better than the shelter of the cocoon. The ways of invention and discovery also follow the course of freely accepted discipline and intellectual standards. Struggle is the nucleus of human life. Struggle creates tension and tension at times makes man behave in an aggressive and violent manner. So, to conceive a society which is completely free from violence will amount to asking for the moon. However, we can aim to create a society which is completely free from violence will amount to asking for the moon. However, we can aim to create a society in which aggressive tendencies of man and women are utilized for constructive and creative purposes. The scope for their indulging in violent and destructive behaviour is reduced to the minimum possible limit by ensuring on open climate in the institution and organization.

(*Umrao Singh Chaudhari,* 1998).

Sarvodaya conveys that the good of all is served by promoting the good of the poorest — the lowest and the lost (*P.K. Choubey,* 1993).

Gandhis writings on nonviolence, peace, and education seem uncomfortably naive and simplistic. Those familiar with philosophical literature may be stunned by his seemingly oversimplified, uncritical, and inadequate treatments of difficult, complex, metaphysical, ethical, cultural, and other philosophical concerns relevant to Gandhian views on education.

"Gandhi is an idea of peace. He is concept of non-violence. Gandhi is the name of liberation" [S.N. Prasad, "Gandhi, Nonviolence and Peace": The Associated Publishers, 1995, p. 2]

Gandhi's simplicity has evidenced in his seemingly inadequate philosophical positions on peace-education, can be misleading. It is true that Gandhi is not a philosopher in any specialized sense, and he has little concern for highly abstract and technical philosophical formulations. Nevertheless, beneath the apparent surface of oversimplified, naive and inadequate philosophical affirmations, one often uncovers surprisingly complex, subtle, enigmatic, and contradictory aspects of Gandhi's philosophy. Most important, his reflections on peace-education serve as a challenge and as a catalyst for rethinking dominant positions and have more value for significant philosophical reflection than most mainstream "academic" philosophy.

Basic approach to Gandhi on peace-education is necessarily selective. Because of the sheer volume of Gandhi material, the limited contextual situatedness of any interpreter, and the phenomenological insight that all knowledge is perspectival, any scholar is necessarily selective in his or her focus. This means ignoring or devaluing other Gandhi data, structuring and privileging data in terms of significance, and formulating and arguing for one of a number of possible interpretations of Gandhi on peace-education.

A difficulty in interpreting and applying Gandhi's writings to peace-education arises from complex relations between texts, contexts, and interpretations. Much of this challenge comes from the sheer volume of writings by and about Gandhi. Although he never wrote a lengthy book, The Collected Works of Mahatma Gandhi comes to one hundred volumes of very diverse and highly fragmented newspaper articles, correspondence, speeches, and other writings. One cannot understand Gandhi's various concerns, specific use of language, and diverse formulations without understanding the specific, economic, political, cultural and ethical contexts within which he lived, read texts, and struggled with opponents and alternative approaches. For example, Gandhi describes the Bhagavad-Gita as his favourite scriptural text, and he arrives at his central interpretation of the activist path of karma yoga through a very unusual nonviolent political reading of the Gita. This has to be situated within a context of positive and negative. Jain, Buddhist, Hindu, and Western influences, including a contextualized political struggle for national independence from British colonial domination. True, his formulations of peace-education are shaped by his commitment to the absolute ideals of ahimsa (nonviolence) and satya (truth), but they are also shaped by his changing and conflicted reactions to the specific contextualized structures of a British colonial education. These had socialized "modern" Indians to adopt Western models and to devalue or feel ashamed of traditional Hindu and other Indian values.

What this means is that in formulating Gandhi's views on peace-education, we must become aware of complex and dynamic interactions of texts and contexts and the creative, open-ended project of interpreting meaning. This is true of the interpretative horizon of meaning within which Gandhi lived, provided linguistic formulations, and interpreted meaning; and it is true of our own linguistic interpretative horizon within which we are contextually situated, read Gandhi's writings, and formulate our own interpretations of meaning. Our reading of Gandhi's texts on peace-education, our symbolic and other linguistic formulations, and our intepretations of meaning involve the complex, dynamic, and often contradictory interactions and mediations between two horizons of meaning. Gandhi's contextualized textual world of meaning and our own.

There is not one static or absolutely true view of real Mahatma Gandhi. This is because we are presented with multiple Gandhi's and multiple Gandhian Views of peace-education. In fact, every reading of Mahatma Gandhi becomes a re-reading and every interpretation becomes a reinterpretation and every formulation a reformulation. We get ourselves involved in a creative, dynamic, open-ended process of contenstation in which we consider and argue of different Gandhian views of peace-education in terms of consistency, adequacy, significance and contemporary relevance.

Many essentialist interpretations uphold a very rigid, conservative, reactionary Gandhi, who idealizes premodern societies and uses absolute ethical and spiritual norms to reject alcohol consumption, meat eating, materialism, consumerism, modern medicine, technology, industrialization, globalization, and other features of a violent modern West. Other essentialist interpretations uphold a very radical, forward-looking Gandhi, who is engaged in a revolutionary project of using absolute ethical and spiritual norms to transform human relations in the direction of nonviolence compassion, love, peace and truth.

Truly, Gandhiji's service to Britain has been not much less great than his service of our country. He inspired the people of India to keep the struggle on a spiritual plane that was above the level of sheet politics. Thus non-violent revolution and the great weapon of "Satyagraha" is a characteristic of Indian accomplishment. This slowly found a new field of action in India's domestic life in the form of self-employment, untouchability, dignity of labour, respect for all religions, encouragements to small industries, gram-swaraj, the Bhoodan movement which taught the value of not to hoard and to give our excess to our less fortunate brethren. Gandhiji's theory of non-violence has been put into practice by India, whether it is in relation with its neighbouring counties dealing with terrorism or even internal strife. If India were ever to fail to live up to this Indian heritage, it would be a poor lookout to mankind as a whole. This is great spiritual responsibility tests on India

Broad minded approach to non violence, satyagraha and spiritual reality is a characteristic of Indian philosophy and its focal point is peace all over the world, This can be continued by teaching people of every age group to be self-satisfied, have control over their emotions, tolerance and love towards others. This starts from every home and flows on to religious sects, to society, to state, to nation and then to the world, This is the crux of Peace-education. Of course, we may have very different concepts and definitions of peace-education in Europe, Asia, Africa or America. But there is a consensus on at least four challenges for peace-education. These are:

1. The condemnation of past, present and menacing wars,
2. The resistance against all firms of violence,
3. The constructive dealing with conflicts, and
4. The development of vision of peace and peaceful living together.

Mahatma Gandhi has said — "Non-violence is not a garment to be put on and off at will. Its seat is in the heart and it must be an inseparable part of our very being."

One of Gandhiji"s major social evil is "education without character". He emphasized that one main goal of education should be character building which focuses on strength, fearlessness, courage, virtue, truth, non violence and selfless work. But, unfortunately, Gandhi is murdered each day, each moment is assassinated. Masses of India are still exploited. Even intellectuals are not free [excluding a few exception] from the organized authority of concerned institution of society. Gandhiji's life is the hope for humanity and inspiration for the future. His whole life was dedicated to the cause of eradicating social discrimination and economic disparity. He belonged to all human races. He said — "I will not hurt Germany or England for the sake of serving my country. That kind of selfish patriotism would be unworthy of truely civilized human being."

It was Gandhi's conviction that individuals — of whom the nations and global communities are constituted — must have priority in any scheme of reform or reconstruction.

The cultivation of non-violence by the individual and the establishment of non-exploitative economy at different levels will lead eventually to the emergence of what he calls non-violent nationalism. Ultimately, these non-violent Nations will function under a world federation on the basis of economic independence. Voluntary efforts, development within, equality for all, decentralization on all spheres, general disarmament, common good of all, amicable settlements of disputes, impartial media and mutual sense of service are must for creating a happy peaceful society.

Gandhi is one with Thoureau's principle that "Government is best which governs the least". To quote Gandhi: "I look upon an increase in the power of the state with the greatest fear because...

it does the greatest harm to mankind by destroying individuality which lies at the root of all progress. In order to our emergence of authoritarianism, Gandhi looks forward to the emergence of a world where "no state has his military".

Socio-economic decentralization is yet another corrective measure to curb undemocratic tendencies. Gandhi's global vision moves upward from the individual and a federation of village republics to an international federation of nations in a society marked by voluntary cooperation and decentralization which certainly leads to effective global village.

Concludingly, it may be said that Gandhiji struggled and fought for peace, which creates creativity and universal brotherhood in the globe. He staunchly worked for the welfare of all. Gandhiji's peace and non-violence are like head and tail of the same coin. He will ever be remembered as father of peace in the globe. If each one sincerely follows Gandhian thoughts, these will certainly be eternal peace on this good earth!

❖ Martin Luther

Martin Luther was born in Atlanta on 15th January, 1929. Both his father and grandfather were Baptist preachers who had been actively involved in the civil rights movement. In 1958, Martin Luther wrote a book entitled "Stride Towards Freedom." The book described and explained his views on non-violence and direct action. The book was to have a considerable influence on the civil rights movement. His non-violent strategy was adopted by black students all over the Deep South. This included the activities of the Freedom Riders in their campaign against segregated transport.

Martin Luther travelled the country making speeches and inspiring people to become involved in civil rights movement.

On 30th January, 1956, a bomb was thrown into the house of Martin Luther King. He wrote about the incident in his book, *Stride Toward Freedom* (1958).

I was immediately driven home. As we neared the scene, I noticed hundreds of people with angry faces in front of the house. The policemen were trying, in their usual rough manner, to clear the streets, but they were ignored by the crowd. One Negro was saying to a policeman, who was attempting to push him aside: "I ain't gonna move nowhere. That's the trouble now; you white folks is always pushin' us around. Now you got your .38 and I got mine; so let's battle it out." As I walked toward the front of the porch, I realized that many people were armed. Nonviolent resistance was on the verge of being transformed into violence.

In this atmosphere, I walked out to the porch and asked the crowd to come to order. In less than a moment there was complete silence. Quietly I told them that I was all right and that my wife and baby were all right. "Now let's not become panicky," I continued. "If you have weapons, take them home; if you do not have them, please do not seek to get them. We cannot solve this problem through retaliatory violence. We must meet violence with nonviolence. Remember the words of Jesus: 'He who lives by the sword will perish by the sword.' " I then urged them to leave peacefully. "We must love our white brothers," I said, "no matter what they do to us. We must make them know that we love them. Jesus still cries out in words that echo across the centuries: 'Love your enemies; bless them that curse you; pray for them that despitefully use you.' This is what we must live by. We must meet hate with love. Remember," I ended, "if I am stopped, this movement will not stop, because God is with the movement. Go home with this glowing faith and this radiant assurance."

At the age of thirty-five, Martin Luther King, Jr., was the youngest man to have received the Nobel Peace Prize. When notified of his selection, he announced that he would turn over the prize money of $54,123 to the furtherance of the civil rights movement.

On the evening of April 4, 1968, while standing on the balcony of his motel room in Memphis, Tennessee, where he as to lead a protest march in sympathy with striking garbage workers of that city, he was assassinated.

Martin Luther was fully a man of non-violence. In one of his speeches, he said — "We are seeking things in a democratic way." Almost in all the meetings of Martin Luther, there was a military discipline combined with emotion!

❖ Martin Luther King's Legacy of Peace

He was best known as a civil rights leader, but he was also an activist for the alleviation of poverty and a strong critic of the US war in Vietnam. King, following in the footsteps of Gandhi, stood firmly for nonviolence and peace, and against the advice of many of his supporters spoke out powerfully against the war.

In the forty years that have passed since King's assassination, his commitment to peace and strong statements against the US war in Vietnam have often been omitted in recalling his legacy. But today, as the US fights another illegal and immoral war in a distant land, again killing young Americans and hundreds of thousands of civilians, his fierce opposition to the Vietnam War should be remembered for the lessons he left us.

Just three weeks after the assassination, his widow, Coretta Scott King, gave a speech in New York City that Dr. King had been scheduled to give. In that speech, she read from some notes that Dr. King had scribbled in preparation for the speech, "Ten Commandments on Vietnam." With small changes, these could be called, "Ten Commandments on Iraq." They go to the very roots of our culture of militarism.

These are Dr. King's "Ten Commandments on Vietnam," written shortly before his untimely death:

1. Thou shalt not believe in a military victory.
2. Thou shalt not believe in a political victory.
3. Thou shalt not believe that the Vietnamese people love us.
4. Thou shalt not believe that the Saigon government has the support of the people.
5. Thou shalt not believe that the majority of the South Vietnamese look upon the Viet Cong as terrorists.
6. Thou shalt not believe the figures of killed enemies or killed Americans.
7. Thou shalt not believe that the generals know best.
8. Thou shalt not believe that the enemies' victory means communism.
9. Thou shalt not believe that the world supports the United States.
10. Thou shalt not kill.

Dr. King knew how to speak truth to power, and in his courage and commitment lay his own power. Had he lived, he would have been an imposing force for peace in America and the world. His commandments confront the comfortable lies our leaders tell about war, which are so widely accepted without questioning.

❖ Nelson Mandela

Nelson Rolihlahla Mandela was born in Transkei, South Africa, on July 18th 1918. His father was Chief Henry Mandela of the Tembu Tribe. Rolihlahla Mandela became the first member of his family to attend a school, where his teacher Miss Modingane gave him the English name "Nelson".

Mahatma Gandhi influenced a lot Mandela's approach and subsequently the methods of succeeding generation of South African anti-apartheid activities. Mandela later took part in the 29th-30th Jan. 2007 Conference in New Delhi making the 100th anniversary of Gandhi's introduction of Satyagraha [non-violent resistance] in South Africa.

In 1993, Nelson Mandela was awarded the Nobel Peace Prize. This is hardly surprising considering the work he has done. A nobel peace prize is not won lightly. Under Nelson Mandela's leadership, the injustice of apartheid has been addressed and to a large extent ended [at least politically and on paper].

There is no peace without equality and this is a message Nobel peace prize Mandela has sought all his life to bring through to the people of South Africa and the people of the world.

In his acceptance of the Nelson Mandela Nobel Peace Prize, he had this to say — These countless human beings, both inside and outside our country, had the nobility of spirit to stand in the path of tyranny and injustice, without seeking selfish gain. "They recognised that an injury to one is an injury to all and therefore acted together in defence of justice and a common human decency." In his own efforts, Mandela recognised those of others and the work that they had done to bring peace to his people and all humanity.

Nelson Mandela was awarded the Nobel Peace Prize along with Frederick William de Kirk for "their work for the peaceful termination of the apartheid regime, and for laying the foundations for a new democratic South Africa". These are no small words of praise.

In a life that symbolizes the triumph of the human spirit, Nelson Mandela accepted the 1993 Nobel Peace Prize on behalf of all South Africans who suffered and sacrificed so much to bring peace to the land.

Nelson Mandela was inaugurated as President of the South Africa on May 10th 1994. In his inaugural speech he said —

"We dedicate this day to all the heroes and heroines in this country and the rest of the world who sacrificed in many ways and surrendered their lives so that we could be free. Their dreams have become reality. Freedom is their reward. We are both humbled and elevated by the honour and privilege that you, the people of South

Africa, have bestowed on us, as the first President of a united, democratic, non-racial and non-sexist government."

"We understand it still that there is no easy road to freedom. We know it well that none of us acting alone can achieve success. We must therefore act together as a united people, for national reconciliation, for nation building, for the birth of a new world. Let there be justice for all. Let there be peace for all. Let there be work, bread, water and salt for all. Let each know that for each the body, the mind and the soul have been freed to fulfil themselves. Never, never and never again shall it be that this beautiful land will again experience the oppression of one by another and suffer the indignity of being the skunk of the world. Let freedom reign."

Nelson Mandela stepped down in 1999 after one term as President; but for him there had been no real retirement. He set up three foundations bearing his name:

1. The Nelson Mandela Foundation,
2. The Nelson Mandela Children's Fund, and
3. The Mandela-Rhodes Foundation.

Nelson Mandela never wavered in his devotion to democracy, equality and learning. Despite terrible provocation, he has never answered racism with racism. His life has been an inspiration, in South Africa and throughout the world, to all who are oppressed and deprived, to all who are opposed to oppression and deprivation.

> *" I have fought against white domination, and I have fought against black domination. I have cherished the ideal of a democratic and free society in which all persons live together in harmony and with equal opportunities. It is an ideal which I hope to live for and to achieve. But if needs be, it is an ideal for which I am prepared to die."*
>
> — ***Nelson Mandela***

♣♣♣

5

TOWARDS A CULTURE OF PEACE

CULTURE OF PEACE

Peace-education is an integral part of the work of United Nations. Through a humanising process of teaching and learning, Peace-educators facilitate human development. They strive to counteract the dehumanisation of poverty, prejudice, discrimination, rape, violence and war. Originally aimed at eliminating the possibility of global extinction through nuclear war, peace-education currently addresses the broader objective of building a culture of peace. In this global effort, progressive educators worldwide are teaching the values, the Human Rights, Elimination of all sort of discrimination against women, the convention on the Rights of the Child, the World Declaration on Education For All, and many others.

UNICEF and UNESCO are particularly active advocates of education for peace. UNICEF describes peace-education as schooling and other educational initiatives that:

- Function as 'zones of peace', where children are safe from violent conflict.
- Uphold children's basic rights as outlined in the CRC.
- Develop a climate that models peaceful and respectful behaviour among all members of the learning community.
- Demonstrate the principles of equality and non-discrimination in administrative policies and practices.
- Draw on the knowledge of peace-building that exists in the community, including means of dealing with conflict that are effective, non-violent, and rooted in the local culture.
- Handle conflicts in ways that respect the rights and dignity of all involved.
- Integrate an understanding of peace, human rights, social justice and global issues throughout the curriculum whenever possible.
- Provide a forum for the explicit discussion of values of peace and social justice.
- Use teaching and learning methods that stress participation, Cupertino, problem-solving and respect for differences.
- Enable children to put peace-making into practice in the educational setting as well as in the wider community.
- Generate opportunities for continuous reflection and professional development of all educators in relation to issues of peace, justice and rights. (Peace-education in UNICEF Working Paper Series, July 1999)

Much of the work of UNESCO is centred on the promotion of education for peace, human rights, and democracy. The notion of a "culture of peace" was first elaborated for UNESCO at the International Congress on Peace in the Minds of Men, held at Yamoussoukro, Cote d'Ivoire, in 1989. The Yamoussoukro declaration called on UNESCO to 'construct a new vision of peace by developing a peace culture based on the universal values of respect for life, liberty, justice, solidarity, tolerance, human rights and equality between women and men' and to promote education and research for a this vision. (UNESCO and a Culture of Peace, UNESCO Publishing, 1995).

Underlying all of this work in the field of peace-education are the efforts of committed educators, researchers, activists, and members of global civil society. Acting in partnership with the United Nations and its Specialised Agencies, Non-governmental Organisations (NGOs), educational institutions, and citizen networks have advanced education for peace by linking ideals with extensive research and practice. The Hague Agenda for Peace and Justice for the 21st Century (UN Document: Ref A/54/98), is a significant example of such work. One of the first principles of this document is the necessity of instituting systematic education for peace. According to the Agenda, their Global Campaign for Peace-education aims to "support the United Nations Decade for a Culture of Peace and Non-violence for the Children of the World and to introduce peace and human rights education into all educational institutions, including medical and law schools."

"A culture of peace will be achieved when citizens of the world understand global problems, have the skills to resolve conflicts and struggle for justice non-violently, live by international standards of human rights and equity, appreciate cultural diversity, and respect the Earth and each other. Such learning can only be achieved with systematic education for peace." — *Hague Appeal for Peace Global Campaign for Peace-education.*

The International Peace Research Association, founded with support from UNESCO, has a Peace-education Commission that brings together educators working to promote a culture of peace. The Peace-Education Network, based in London, also works alongside the UN in promoting peace through education. Overall, the participation of global civil society in building a culture of peace is essential. Get connected!

Because the year 2000 is the International Year for the Culture of Peace (UN Doc A/RES/52/15) and the period 2001-2010 is the International Decade for a Culture of Peace and Non-Violence for the Children of the World (UN Doc A/RES/53/25), the UN Cyberschoolbus Peace-education site joins the global movement to build and sustain a culture of peace through education.

Peace-education brings together multiple traditions of pedagogy, theories of education and international initiatives for the advancement of human development through learning. It is fundamentally, dynamic, interdisciplinary, multicultural and grows out of work of educators such as John Dewey, Maria Montessori, Paulo Freire, Johan Galtung and many more.

Building on principles and practices that have evolved over time, responding to different historical circumstances, peace-education aims to cultivate the knowledge, skills, and attitudes needed to achieve and sustain a global culture of peace. Understanding and transforming violence is central. The following diagram helps visualise the core relationship between violence and peace.

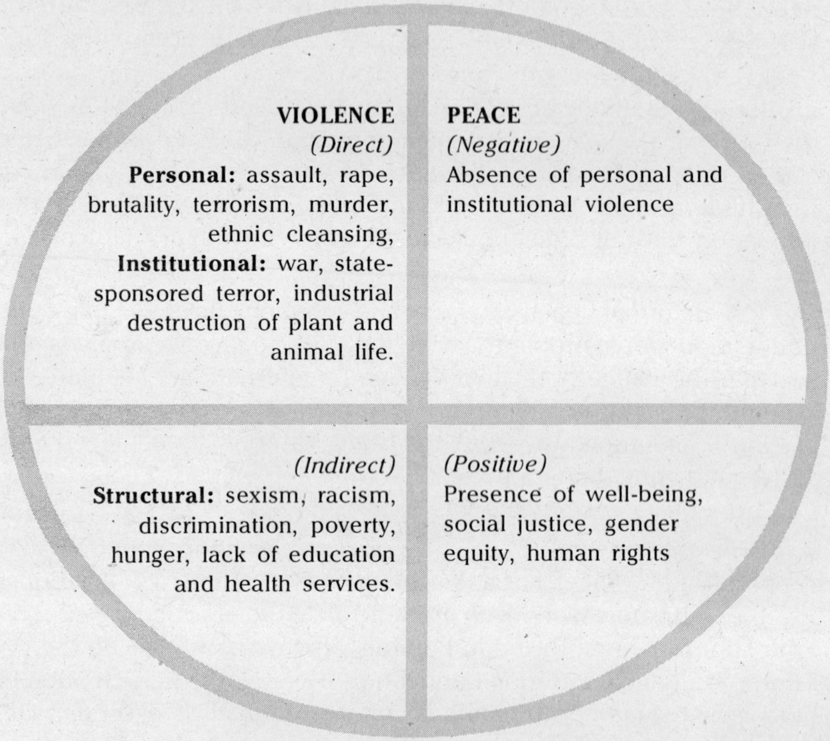

Source: http://www.un.org/cyberschoolbus/peace/content.htm

Peace-education aims not to reproduce but to transform. It consists of people "consciously striving to educate their successors not for existing state of affairs but so as to make possible a future better humanity." [John Dowey "Democracy and Education"]. And with this task comes significant challenges and opportunities for all involved.

One way to meet the challenges of peace-education is to build bridges of support among key participants. Just as learning takes place in a broader social context and not exclusively in schools or classrooms, so peace-education relies on families, communities, and social networks to affect positive and lasting change. The notion "think globally, act locally" is central to educating for a Culture Of Peace, in that it links theory with practice, international issues to individual efforts.

As a peace educator, you need not work alone. The international peace-education community is active and growing through networks, publications, global campaigns, national initiatives, and international programs. Concerned Citizens, educators and activists of all ages around the world are promoting and building peace through education. Get connected!

Source: http://www.un.org/cyberschoolbus/peace/content.htm

A culture of peace will be achieved when citizens of the world understand global problems, have the skills to resolve conflicts and struggle for justice non-violently, live by international standards of human rights and equity, appreciate cultural diversity and respect the Earth and each other.

Peace-making, peace-keeping, and peace-building are complex and important responses to the proliferation of violent conflict. The root of these approaches lies in the basic knowledge and commitment to the practice of non-violence and critical thinking. When we eliminate violence as an option for resolving conflicts, we make room for creative alternatives. Co-operation, critical thinking, communication and problem-solving become essential tools. Conflict itself can be viewed as an opportunity for growth and expanded communication rather than a precursor to violence and a threat to dignity, security and life. Peace educators are developing tools to help transform the current "culture of violence" in which hurt and harm are advocated and glorified to a "culture of peace" in which the preservation of life and human dignity are the central guiding principles for living together in a secure world.

While UNICEF and UNESCO are active advocates of education for peace, Non-Governmental Organizations [NGOs], educational institutions and citizen networks have advanced education for peace by linking ideas with extensive research and practice. The Hague Agenda for Peace and Justice for the 21st Century highlights the need for instructing systematic education for peace. According to the Agenda, their global campaign for Peace-education aims to support the United Nations decade for a culture of peace and non-violence for the children of the world and to introduce peace and human rights education into all educational institutions, including mental and law schools.

The International Peace Education Association founded with support from UNESCO has a Peace Education Commission that brings together educators working to promote a culture of peace. Peace Education Network based in London also works alongside the UN in promoting peace through education. Overall, the participation of global civil society in building a culture of peace is essential.

Peace-education does not teach students what to think, but how to think critically. In the process, its holistic and participatory approach may conflict with more traditional curriculum. Peace-education aims not to produce but to transform. It consists of people consciously striving to educate pupils to make possible a future better humanity (John Dewey, *Democracy and Education*). And with this task comes significant challenges and opportunities for all involved. One way to meet the challenges of peace-education is to build bridges of support among key participants. Just as learning takes place in a broader social context, so peace-education relies on families, communities and social networks to affect positive and lasting change.

In a period of transition and accelerated change marked by the expression of intolerance, manifestations of racial and ethnic hatred, the upsurge of terrorism in all its forms and manifestations, discrimination, war and violence towards those regarded as 'other' and the growing disparities between rich and poor, at international and national levels alike, action strategies must aim both at ensuring fundamental freedoms, peace, human rights, and democracy and at promoting sustainable and equitable economic and social development all of which have an essential part to play in building a culture of peace.

As stated in the preamble of the Constitution of UNESCO [the United Nations Educational, Scientific and Cultural Organization], "Since war begins in the minds of men, it is the minds of men that the defences of peace must be constructed." The knowledge, skills and attitudes needed to prevent violence and promote the non-violent resolution of conflict are central to the process of educating for a culture of peace. A summarised by one organisation:

A culture of peace will be achieved when citizens of the world understand global problems, have the skills to resolve conflicts and struggle for justice non-violently, live by international standards of human rights and equity, appreciate cultural diversity, and respect the Earth and each other. 'Culture of Peace' brings together multiple traditions of pedagogy, theories of education and international initiatives for the advancement of human development. It is fundamentally dynamic, interdisciplinary and multicultural and grows out of the work of educators such as Joh Dewey, Maria Montessari, Paulo Frieire, Johan Gultang and many others.

Building on principles and practices that have evolved over time, responding to different historical circumstances, peace-education aims to cultivate the knowledge, skills, and attitudes needed to achieve and sustain a global culture of peace. Understanding and transforming violence is central.

Peace is understand not only as the absence of traditional forms of direct violence, but also as a positive presence. Educating for and about all aspects of peace constitutes the Culture of Peace.

As its meeting in Mach 1999, the Executive Board of Education International decided to support the United Nations Year for a Culture of Peace.

The first step in the Education International was to promote Education for a Culture of peace. The appeal for the Year of a Culture of Peace, identifies the component parts of the work that governments, intergovernmental organizations, NGOs, Education-establishments and the media are called upon to support.

A Culture of Peace goes to the heart of fundamental human rights; and the key components are the issues of social justice, literacy, economic justice, health sustainable environmental development, equality and non-discrimination. Putting a special focus on the work that must be done in education to teach the principles that underlie a culture of peace requires the curricula at all levels that include active listening, dialogue, mediation skills and cooperative learning. It requires a dynamic, long-term process that provides pupils as well as adults with an understanding of and respect for universal values and rights.

Education International invites all the member-organizations to join on the promotion of Education for a Culture of Peace.

In the best of our knowledge, it is a fact to state that alone, we cannot change a great deal, but millions of education personnel. Working together as a part of the campaign to provide Education for a Culture of Peace, can make a difference. This can happen only because a human being is the supreme creation of God; but the question is whether he or she is maintaining his or her supremacy or not. In the present prevalent materialistic and scientific age, men and animals are alike it almost all the activities. *i.e.*, eating, drinking, sleeping and making only one thing that differentiates a human being from an animal is the mental faculty bestowed by God to him or her. Man can ponder over what is bad and good, what is wrong and right, where the animal cannot. Man has become materialistic and money-minded and lost the faith in God. He thinks for his own benefit and does not bother for other' happiness or sadness. So too, we are losing our cultural values. In fact, India is known for its culture but today we see that the cultural heritage of India has lapsed. No doubt, our civilization has made progress because of technological advancement; yet, at the same time, there is lot of loss of cultural values. We are blindly following the Western Culture and feel proud about it! We are overhead the vote of our soul and do not give any importance to the voice of our conscience. In fact, humanity is the essence of all religion. But this fact has been forgotten unfortunately. The lapse of our cultural values are so fast that the day is not far when we will endanger our existence, we, as teachers, have therefore to take a strong step in protecting our cultural values and try sincerely to maintain a culture of peace!

"It is not enough to send peace-keeping forces to separate warring parties. It is not enough to engage in peace-building efforts after societies have been ravaged by conflicts. It is not enough to conduct preventive diplomacy. All of this is essential work, but we want enduring results. We need, in short, a Culture of Peace."

— ***Koffi Annan***
United Nations Secretary General

The Culture of Peace needs to start with children and through education. Children and young people are the future of mankind. There is a need to invest in these children and our future. Is peace a teachable process? Yes! An education system can develop attitudes and skills to prevent conflicts. Instead of just absence of war, Peace is now seen as involving cooperation and non-violent social change aimed at creating more equitable just structure in a society [Positive Peace]. Culture is how we live, how we think, how we speak, how we behave. When we do all these with positive values, then, we live in a Culture of Peace. It brings benefit to the self and others. Peace is a way of being, doing and living in society that we can teach, develop and best of all improve upon. Peace is living in harmony amidst diversity. Where and when we adopt a common platform of Positive Values, peace is not only absence of conflicts but requires a positive, dynamic, anticipatory process where dialogue is encouraged and conflicts are solved in a spirit of mutual understanding cooperation. The power of peace is to change future headlines from "violence increases again" to "violence diminish."

According to U.N.. Peace Declaration Article 1 —

Peace Means –Full respect for and promotion of all human rights and fundamental freedom.

Respect for and promotion of right to development.

Respect for and promotion of rights of everyone to freedom of expression, opinion and information.

❖ What exactly Peace means?

Peace means much more than the absence of war. Peace is considered as a set of values, attitudes and modes of behaviour promoting the peaceful settlement and conflict and the quest for mutual understanding.

❖ Role of Education

Education can help to overcome conflict. Conflict is a part of human being's nature. Conflicts are carried over from religious and cultural beliefs. Many of the conflicts are rooted in the "not knowing." The 'not-knowing' can create non-peaceful attitudes. The Peace Foundation encourages peace-education in schools to help students develop —

(*i*) Skills

(*ii*) Attitudes

(*iii*) Knowledge

❖ Skills

- Conflict resolution.
- Cooperation and communication skills.
- Critical thinking to see where there is bias in newspapers, magazines, radio and television.
- Ability to take part response in making decisions.

❖ Attitudes

- A sense of responsibility towards others.
- Respect for human rights.
- Concern for the well being of all people..
- Knowledge about and respect for different cultures.
- A willingness to listen to each other and try to solve problems together.
- A willingness to be well-informed citizens.
- Awareness of the need for honesty, trustworthiness in people behaviour towards each other.

❖ Knowledge

- How conflicts are caused; and the effects that they have on the people.
- How problems can be solved and conflict overcome.
- The work of the various people and agencies who have helped to solve problems and overcome conflicts.
- How the political system works and how people can make their voices heard.
- How everyone in our society can have a fair share of resources.
- Each country's foreign policy, especially how it helps other countries and what our country does in working for World Peace [Peace Foundation , 2004]

Concludingly, it may be said, then, that there is a need for the promotion of peace, and peace is for the continued existence of this planet and for the future of mankind. Peace is teachable. Knowledge of how to achieve peace will help further create a more peaceful world and create harmony among all in the future.

❖ Spirituality and Peace

'ISO Upanishad' teaches us that one who views all beings as belonging to the 'Atman' and also see the Atman in all the beings, such a person ceases to have hatred towards any being.

Mahatma Gandhi had learnt in his childhood from his mother Potli Bai and his neighbourers, two Indian Maxims:

"There is nothing higher than truth" and "Non-violence is the highest virtue" [Ahimsa Parmo Dharmah].

With respect from the above said things, if we want to give more instances, we can recall when devotee Prahlad says to his tyrant father: "Within the being of Lord Govinda, who constitutes the soul of all beings, who is the Lord of the world and also one with the world, where is cope for making distinction between friend and for?" **— Vishnu Purana, 1.19.37-38**

Further, it mentions" I do not desire, do or speak evil, thinking all along of the Lord's presence in all beings and in myself ... Knowing that the Lord is involved in all beings, wise men should extend unqualified love and service to all living beings."

— Vishnu Purana, 1.19.7.9

Apart from the Indian heritage, Mahatma Gandhi was also influenced by Socrates, Lord Jesus, and in modern times by Tolstoy, Ruskin, Carlyle, etc. So is the case of Buddha. 'The Light of Asia' gave a touching impression on the life of Buddha. Tolstoy's book "the Kingdom of God is Within You" brought Christianity dearer to the Vedantic idea of man.

Even Islam had an impact on Gandhian non-violence. The very word 'Islam' means 'peace', 'safety' and 'salvation'. Hence the common Muslim salutation 'salam alikum' means 'peace be on you'. The Islam prefer non-violence to violence!

But what is Peace-education? Answer is deceptively simple. Peace-education is the education with a focus on peace. But what is education? And what is peace? Generally, or institutionally, education is the process by which a culture maintains itself across generations, individually, it is a process whereby an educator attempts to improve an educatee using a morally acceptable process. The same basic issues and questions that have occupied eductors occupy peace-education formal vs.. informal, top down vs. bottom top, separate subject vs. across the curriculum, etc. There is, therefore, no fixed, single methodology and no consensus on content. The variety of approaches may be reflected in the variety of technology: peace-education, peace studies, peach research, disarmament education, defense education would order studies, global education conflict resolution studies, international studies, and even multicultural education. On the other hand, it is possible that some philosophies of education are mutually exclusive, and by failing to recognize this, and including everything that is called peace-education in the curriculum, some of our efforts will be neutralised and our work rendered meaningless. What, then, is the appropriate approach to peace-education? How compatible are the alternative approaches?

❖ Blending Science and Spirituality for World Peace

We all know that science is the backbone of human society. In fact, modern technology and science has brought great change to the life of human beings. Science has dragged a luxurious and comfortable life-style to the people of 21st century. However, at the same time, it is noticeable that these people of modern age have faced various problems such as extremist, dacoit, kidnapping, rape, hijacking, murder, cheating, etc. Now, at any moment in any part of the world, people easily succumb to death in bomb-blast, assassination, rioting by extremist cheating, robbing, kidnapping, molestation, etc. are also some easily found characteristics of a city. Now, in such a modern age, for the survival of the human race, we need Culture of Peace in the world. Spirituality help grow up inner feelings of human beings. It teaches people to love every object in the world. Hence, blending of science and spirituality is very much urgent for survival of human race, and also along with this a story need for the development of Culture of Peace.

❖ Culture of Peace and Building a Better World

Society is made up of people with different wishes, resources, idealogies and cultural preconditions. An active concept of peace looks at how the interaction between people takes place without leading to violent confrontations.

Peace-education is not just what happens in school for academic purpose; and education for culture of peace is about how people can help build the future and make our world a more peaceful place of living. Schools can cultivate the culture of peace through humanistic management approach, improving human relations, developing good attitudes in students as well as teachers, facilitating socialization, improving discipline, developing, creativity, etc. Hence, culture of peace is the only hope for violence-free society as it promotes mutual understandings, culture of peace through sharing responsibilities, tolerance and solving conflicts.

All religions teach that God is in Man and Man is possessed of the power to choose between good and evil. The "good" is peace and 'evil' is war and terrorism.

❖ Blending A Culture of Peace through Education — Science as well as Spirituality

Peace building is one of the biggest challenges faced by people who sincerely seek the progress of society. The culture of peace is, at its core, an ethical approach to life, recognizing that the world is experiencing a fundamental crisis. A new vision of peace can be constructed by developing a peace culture based on the universal values of life, liberty, justice, solidarity, tolerance and human rights and equality between woman. Violence can be prevented through a more tolerant common global ethic. With education as an essential tool at all levels the culture of peace can be fostered shunning violence and accepting cooperation and social justice. Just as wars begin in the minds of individuals so must peace — UNESCO, thus seeks to build the defenses of peace in the mind of individuals.

Education to children from early ages to adulthood can help to resolve any dispute peacefully in a spirit of respect for human dignity, tolerance and non-discrimination.

Creating and nurturing a culture of peace is a social movement which requires a profound transformation in outthinking and acting which cannot be achieved overnight or in a decade. Action is urgently needed to build a just world if humanity is to survive. There is no time left for anything but to make peace work. The call of the hour is to encourage every effort, aimed at building a culture of peace through education. Since no education is worth its name which does not inculcate the qualities necessary for living graciously, harmoniously and efficiently with one's fellow men. Passion for peace must be kindled in the heart and mind of our pupils since early childhood. Only when this responsibility of doing good deeds and good actions is kindled in the heart of every child and every man will changes and transformation in our lives takes place and peace and harmony prevail in our families, schools and the society at large.

The culture of peace should not be considered as the technical solution to every world problem, rather it supplies the moral foundation for establishing a better individual and global order — a vision that can lead individuals away from despair and society away from chaos. Though religion does not have an ownership formation of moral standards, religions are especially well placed to advance the standards of a culture of peace. India is on the move with the promise of a new renaissance and modernization in education gabed on moral and spiritual values on one hand and science and technology on the other, since conflicts can lead us to nowhere.

Peace is a state of harmony with the absence of hostility. Peace is thus a relationship between two people characterized by respect, justice and goodwill. According to the words of Albert Einstein — "Peace cannot be kept by force. It can only be achieved by understanding." Therefore, we need to create avenues for people to come together, understand participate and contribute to sustainable peace and co-existence. Hefsat Abiola said, "Peace comes from being able to contribute the best that we have and all that we are toward creating a world that supports everyone. But it is also securing the space for others to contribute the best that they have and all that they are."

Therefore, in all earnestness we should give our best to attain peace that is the most basic starting point of our success. Only then we can build a just world for humanity to survive through a culture of peace.

Concludingly, it may be said that, alone, we cannot change a great deal; but millions of education personnel, working together as a part of a campaign to provide Education for a Culture of Peace, can make a difference.

Let us now try to lay down certain strategies for developing a Culture of Peace.

❖ A Few Strategies for Developing a Culture of Peace [Teachers to note]

1. Create a project for Peace that is unique to your own community.
2. Organize a Peace-Walk that culminates in visiting a hospital, a nursing home or a prison.
3. Work out a plan that will bring love, harmony and gratitude into one's own life and in doing so help to bring Peace to the world at large.
4. Plan for leading a series of group meditations for Peace.
5. Try to have a Peace concert or a poetry-reading concerning ideas on Peace.
6. Plan integrational Peace-building activities such as planting a tree.
7. Give your students an opportunity to discuss about peace.
8. Try to create an energy that will be creative and constructive for emphasizing peace.
9. Plan for a Culture of Peace week.
10. Organize the celebrations of Culture of Peace in your school.
11. Try to provide an in-service training in your school for developing Peace-Strategies.
12. Plan to rebuild those personal relationships that have been damaged because of one reason or other.
13. Try to concentrate in engaging your pupils in dialogues with such pupils who are rejected by others (parents, friends, neighbours, etc.)

Summing up, it may be said as follows —

The narrow view of peace defines it as the absence of violence, but in a wider sense it means the removal of structural and cultural violence. Gandhi, envisages peace as far more than the absence of war & violence. It is a state of positive and constructive world view and world order. We need each other. All of us are interdependent. Here comes the role of education, which teaches, trains, indoctrinates and educates us to live in harmony with others. The international commission on education in the 21st century lays emphasis on "Living Together" as one of the pillars of Education. National Curriculum Framework — 2005 also advocates Education for Peace and suggest peace activities and strategies. In India, the National Focus Group on Education for Peace (2006) states that Education for Peace be integrated in the teacher education, text book, school setting, evaluation etc. A culture of peace can be developed only when the prospective teachers are educated how to inculcate it among the students. Let us work together in identifying the peace building strategies and practices.

Across the world, Peace-education programs are gaining popularity, as states, international agencies and civil society organizations increasingly recognize the importance of such education. However, with this growing recognition, there are increasing contestations over both the broader objectives and the specificities of carrying out peace-education programs. The widespread interest in preparing individuals for peace on earth makes us resort to the teaching-learning process. The inevitability of this emphasis upon education for peace has arisen not only from the need to educate the public opinion of the scourges of war, its prodigality or the danger of total annihilation etc., but also from the necessity to promote understanding, acceptance and friendship among all peoples and nations, and to strengthen respect for human rights and fundamental freedoms.

Peace-education asserts that the reality of war is created by cultural and educational manipulations by reinforcing group identification and creating images of the enemies and the possible for them. The tendency to dehumanize the enemy is due to the denial of the human values resulting in killing of innocent civilians including children and woman. It is peace-education which inculcates and builds love, friendship and international understanding. We intend to teach the young minds valuable contribution towards peaceful society. The society which upholds the values of equality, solidarity, freedom, democratic inclination, tolerance, care and respect for others and willingness to change. If we intend to create a peaceful society we must renew our educational society, which has no scope for inculcating the human values. Our examination system needs to be re-examined which in fact fosters cut-throat competition; rather than examining the right type of the potential of the individual. Our environment, the school, playground, home and our media focus more on violence rather than peace.

A culture of peace will be achieved when citizens of the world understand global problems; have the skills to resolve conflicts constructively, know and live by international standards of human rights, gender and racial equality, appreciate cultural diversity and respect the integrity of the Earth. Such learning cannot be achieved without intentional; sustained and systematic education for peace.

Furthermore, it may be said, then, that let there be not just the efforts putforth for peace-education; but, Peace-Development Education. In order to achieve this, the organic wholeness of the human being is very much essential. Today, man has completely broken up from within; and this inner disintegration is reflected in the disorganized state of human system at all levels. This disharmony tends to disturbances. Therefore, there is a need for the creation and care of integrated individuals. The culture of peace should be understood as the creation of peaceful, non-violent behavioural patterns. The main indispensable values on which a culture of peace can be built may grouped around such key notions as justice, human rights, democracy, development non-violence and peaceful resolution of conflicts.

All human beings are endowed with the seeds of compassion. When exposed to right conditions at home, school, in society at large, and later perhaps through our pointed efforts in schools (education or training), the seed will flourish. We have seen many examples in life and history that violent behaviour is not inherited, and children of criminals turn out to be good human beings, and by giving a good environment, became useful citizens.

Violence does not appear either as part of our evolutionary legacy or in our genes. It is in our sociological and cultural roots. Individuals are normally ready to adapt to their environment and under normal circumstances refer cooperation to aggressiveness, non-violence to Violence. Unlike any other creature on this planet, humans can learn and understand, without having experienced. They can think themselves into other people's mind; imagine themselves into other people's places. Education and ideas of peace development have the possibility of making things change.

♣♣♣

6

AGENCIES IN PEACE-KEEPING & PEACE-BUILDING

THE CONSTITUTION OF INDIA

Few of the eminent authors have given a definition of constitution in their own way. Dictionary meaning of the word constitution is a system of laws and customs established by the sovereign power of a sate for its own guideline. Word 'Constitution' has emerged form the Latin word 'constituere' meaning to form to establish or to compose. According to Lord Bryce, Constitution is a set of established rules embodying and enacting the practice of Government. Aristotle said — 'Constitution is the way in which citizens who are component parts of the state, are arranged in relation to one another.

Human beings are motivated to work for securing a self-made constitution providing for self-rule. We, Indians opposed British Imperialism in India, demanded the rights to make a constitution for ourselves.

❖ Historical Background

1958 : The British Crown assumed sovereignty over India from the East India Company.

1861 : Executive Council with exclusively of officials later on included non-officials while transacting legislative business.

1885 : Embodiment of National awakening in the country for Indian freedom by A.O. Hume.

1890 : Lord Duffern began to speak ill of Congress. Indians got enraged.

1892 : Indian Councils Act: To widen the basis and expand the functions of Government of India.

1905 : Swaraj Resolution: People in India marched ahead in the national mainstream for securing self-rule and to secure the right to make a constitution themselves.

1909 : Government policy dried to create differences between Hindus and Muslims.

1911 : Jana-Gana-Mana — Song by Ravindranath Tagore.

1915 : Two home leagues launched by Annie Besant.
Lokmanya Tilak (1916)

1916 : Tilak said — "Swaraj is my birthright and I will have it."

1919 : Jallianwala Bagh Massacre increased Indians in every branch of Administration: Gradual development of self government institutions.

1922 : Gandhiji asserted the right of self determination of Indians.

1927 : Non-Cooperative Movement — Simon Commission in 1980.

1928 : M.N. Roy raised the demand.

1930 : Dandi March — A resolution was passed by Motilal Nehru.

1931 : Bhagatsingh and others were hanged by Britishers.

1933 : Nehru insisted for our own constitution

1935 : Government of India Act enactment.

1938 : J. Nehru formulated his demand for a Constituent Assembly.

1939 : British Government demanded co-operation form Indians.

1943 : Gandhiji's fast

1947 : On 15th August, India's Independence was declared.

1950 : 26th Jan. 1950 was declared as the Republic Day of India.

Period 15th Aug. 1947 to 26th Jan. 1950, India's political status was that of a Dominion in the British Common Wealth of Nations.

❖ The Constituent Assembly

After the end of 2nd World War, the British Government through its cabinet mission [1945] accepted the demand for the establishment of a constituent assembly for India for making a constitution of India.

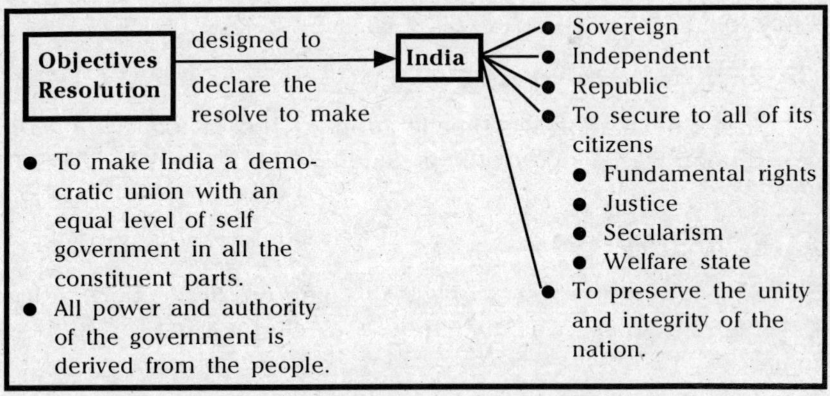

Design of the objectives of the Resolution

N.D. Palmer observed "The document was a statement of the basis on which the new Indian State would be established."

❖ Subsequent Happenings

15th Aug. 1947 India became independent.

14th Aug. 1947 Pakistan was partitioned out of India.

- The Constituents Assembly of India got a sovereign states and started undertaking the task of formulating the Constitution of India with a new zeal and enthusiasm. The accession of many India States to India, made this body more representative. It started working as a fully representative, all powerful and a truly national and representative assembly of all the people of India.
- For the work to be done in a systematic and efficient way, the Constituent Assembly constituted several committees,

which were to report on the subjects, assigned to them. For example: Rules of procedure committee. Finance and Staff committee, Credential committee. Steering committee etc. Such committees laid the foundation in the formation of the constitution of India.

The Drafting Committee

Highly knowledge and experienced people worked on thesis under the Chairmanship of Dr. B.R. Ambedkar. The committee was constituted on 29th Aug. 1947.

Dr. B.R. Ambedkar was the Main architect in making the constitution.

On 26th November 1949

The Constitution was finally adopted and enacted when the constitution was signed by the president of the Constituent Assembly.

26th January 1950

Full Swaraj pledge, people had taken on 26th January 1950. Dr. Rajendra Prasad was unanimously elected as First President of India.

The Constitution has been freely amended according to the procedure laid down in Art 368 more than 92 times, by 2003.

- While making the Constitution, the Drafting committee played a pivotal role. This committee constituted on 29th Aug. 1947 included a very versatile and dynamic Chairman Dr. B.R. Ambedkar, B.L. Mitter, Gopal Swami Iyengar, K.M. Munshi, N. Madhava Rao and many more assisted Dr. B.N. Rao worked as the Chief Constitutional Advisor attached to the committee.
- The Drafting Committee's report (draft) to the Constituent Assembly was submitted on 21st Feb 1948 and a debate was arranged. Based on this, certain changes were made. A new draft was submitted to the Assembly on 4th to 9th Nov. 1948 and from 15th to 17th Nov. each clause was debated and passed.

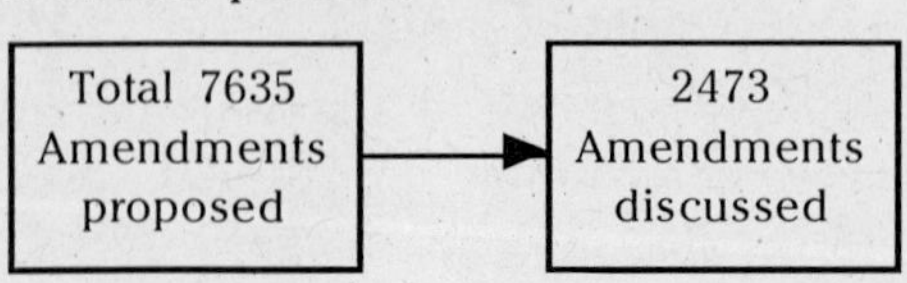

From 14th November 1949 to 26th Nov. 1949, the final debate was held.

Granville Austin says that "The adoption of the constitution of India was the greatest political venture."

Certain proposals came into operation immediately. The Constitution was inaugurated on 26th January 1950.

The Constituent Assembly

- 2 years, 11 months, 18 days for making the Constitution.
- It had 11 plenary sessions. Discussions 114 days held.
- ₹ 64 lakhs spent approximately.

❖ Constitution of India is:

- The Highest
- Most valuablc contribution of the Constituent Assembly to the Indian political system.

Dr. Rajendra Prasad, then President appreciated the work done after the adoption of commission, observed, "I desire to congratulate the Assembly on accomplishing a task of such tremendous magnitude."

Many people appreciated the good work done by Ambedkar and his team which fully reflected the aims and aspirations of all the people of India. Its successful working since 1950 till today makes us to bend our heads to the maturity, wisdom of the founding fathers of the Constitution.

❖ Agencies in Peace Keeping & Peace Building

"Peace is not merely the absence of war but the presence of justice, of law, of order — in short, of government" — Albert Eienstine. Ho vcry true! Peace is a word that is uttered almost as frequently as 'truth', 'beauty' and 'love.' It may be just as elusive to define as the other virtues. Common synonyms for 'peace' include 'amity', 'friendship', 'harmony', 'tranquility', 'response; 'truce', etc. Likewise the peacemaker is the pacifier, mediator, intermediary and intercessor. When we try to talk of violence, it may be said that violence is the expression of physical force against one or more people. Worldwide, violence is used as a tool of manipulation and also in an area of concern for law and police which make attempts to control it.

Violence takes place in different sectors of society such as family, social organization, political and religious fields, industrial organizations, etc. Sometimes violence takes an ugly form causing the loss of human lives and also destruction of property. Hence, the most important requirement is the sustained improvement in all beings and for this, education is the most important means. Progressive development in education is really helpful for nation-building. The entire purpose of education would remain unfulfilled if the aspect of sustainable development as a basic human right is neglected. Education for peace deals with conflicts arising out of aggression or war situation and also arising out of injustice, exploitation and violation of human rights. Education for peace creates a culture of peace, helping to build non-violent education system for the nation's building. Peace-education, thus, can involve everyone such as academic administrators, researchers, teachers, parents, students and the community.

In the words of Betty Peardon — "Peace-education would provide knowledge to be applicable to the problems of reforming and restructuring the present conflicts and violence in human society to make it peaceful, unified and violence-free."

Peace-education may be defined as a process of acquiring the values, the knowledge and developing the attitudes skills and behaviours to live in harmony with oneself, with others and with the natural environment. Peace is the bridge that each one will cross to leave this world behind.

❖ Quotes:

"Disputes may be inevitable, but violence is not. To prevent continued cycles of conflict, education must seek to promote peace and tolerance, no fuel hatred and suspicion".

INICEF 1996, State of the World's Children: Anti War Agenda.

"Help young people integrate their work for peace with every other aspect of life, with their families and communities, religions affiliations, and their jobs and work relationships. The task of inventing peace will require the co-operation of everyone and it will take many years to accomplish".

How You Can Teach Peace: The Seville Statement, 1989.

Let us see still some more quotes.

"Schools are not immune. The disorder of the world surfaces in school in many ways and the very qualities that are needed to address the global crisis are the very same qualities required in school.... Any school can become a community which models how the world may be. For example, each person is respected and honoured; mutuality exists in all relationships; resources are used mindfully and justly ... The values of community, simplicity, helpfulness, creativity, celebration and openness to the spirit bring with them the possibility of a school where people matter and where they can be fulfilled. The same values are those that can contribute to a world where justice, peace and care for the environment are made a priority."

Values and Visions: Spiritual Development and Global Awareness in the Primary School 1993.

"Say very firmly that children learn responsibility best and gain a sense or moral values by discussing, with good guidance from the earliest age, real and controversial issues."

Bernard Crick Education for citizenship and the teaching of democracy in schools. September' 1998.

Peace-education Network is an umbrella group which brings together peace-education practitioners from Anglican Pacifist Fellowship, Peace Museum, Council for Education in World Citizenship (CEWC), Pax Christi, Peace Pledge Union, and Quaker Peace & Service among others.

The Peace Education Resource Centre, India is a Peace Forum. It came into being as a result of the efforts of the concerned students from University of Delhi endorsing "The Hague Agenda for Peace and Justice in the 21st Century." HAP, DU was initially a voluntary students' body. Gradually many like-minded people from various fields joined the body and have led to the formation of Peace Education Resource Centre, India (PERC, India) which is a more formal and structured. Today PERC, India comprises of more than 30 members from different areas of interest, communities and faiths from various parts of the country.

Members of the PERC, India commit themselves to working together on the main objective of promoting and building a culture of Peace through Peace-education. We believe that Peace-education is a participatory holistic process that includes teaching for and about democracy and human rights, nonviolence, social and economic justice, gender equality, environmental sustainability, disarmament, traditional peace practices, international law and human security.

We live in an age of unprecedented violence: locally, nationally and globally. India being the largest democracy in the world, there is a need to make the democratic process present in every area of our lives. Peace in this effort is imperative and respect for human rights by all is the need of the hour. A culture of peace will be achieved when all citizens understand the problems, have the skills to resolve conflict constructively, know and live by international standards of human rights, gender and racial equality, appreciate cultural diversity, respect for individual differences, a sense of tolerance and respect for the integrity of the Earth. Such learning cannot be achieved without intentional, sustained and systematic education for peace.

The members of PERC, India have been actively involved in many activities since its inception in 1998. Community intervention for peaceful resolution of conflict, education for peace and inculcating peace values are some of the activities. Apart from that, numerous talks and seminars have been conducted under its wing. More activities, documentations & trainings are being planned for the near future.

❖ Universal Democratic Society

The preamble of the UN Charter starts with "We the people of the United Nations" to highlight the new concept of world citizenship in a new global order based on "universal democracy." In order to transform the world into a true global common society, it is absolutely necessary to build it, first of all, on the principle of universal democracy.

In retrospect the two main democracies we have experienced — a national, bourgeoisie democracy and a social, proletariat democracy (Communism) — are socially and politically exclusive and divisive systems generating endless conflicts domestically and internationally. These democracies are responsible for exclusive ultra nationalism, ideological division, and hegemonic control which are the root sources of human agony, aggression, exploitation, violation of human rights, and destruction' while obstructing the realization of democracy for all and everywhere.

With the changing spirit of our time, it is now the most urgent task for us to realize the universal democracy and to induce all the people of the world regardless of their nationality to work together as world citizens of a new global community. In order to do this, we must recognize and abide by the principle of human dignity and equal rights of all the people irrespective of their skin colour and languages as provided in the UN Declaration of Human Rights.

Perhaps the United States of America is a model closely approximating an ideal political community which has achieved a democratic federation as a great melting pot accommodating various races, cultures, religions, and interests. When we have achieved a global cooperation society under the United Nations and have established goodwill, exchanges, cooperation, interdependence, coexistence, and co-prosperity among peoples, nations, and states as the matters of routine practice, we will be then successful in establishing firmly the universal democracy.

The Renaissance which resulted in statism, nationalism, doctrinairism, and democracy, and the materialistic view of history by the communists who stressed class struggles were, in reality, all derived from the law of the jungle that justified the materialistic norms in the natural law which emphasized "the strong prey upon the weak" and "the survival of the fittest."

In such social and political systems, the standard of value judgement on right and wrong or good and evil was decided by the logic of power and the outcome of power play. Thus, such systems built upon the belief in power were in a state of constant conflict and struggle due to mutual distrust, deception, subversion, plotting and machination against each other, and war.

In view of this tragic history of human society we had, predominant values and norms of our human society in the forthcoming millennium should be "cultural norms" derived from a universally valid "cultural view of history" replacing the naturalistic norms of the past. Unless we replace the naturalistic norms with the culturalistic norms, we will be perpetually condemned to the fate of conflicts and struggles.

Based on cultural norms, the standard of judging right from wrong and good from evil should as follows:

(*a*) Anything that helps the humanity is "good" and that harms it is "evil".

(*b*) Anything that contributes to the maintenance and development of culture is "good" and that destroys it is "evil".

(*c*) Anything that is consistent with the spirit of the universal democracy is "good" and that is against it is "evil".

(*d*) Anything that fosters cooperative social life is "good" and that obstructs it is "evil."

(*e*) Anything that helps the realization of "good" in the above four categories is "right" or "just" and that prevents it is "wrong" or "unjust."

Unless we establish cultural norms based on the cultural view of history, we human· beings will be forever condemned to repeating the existing pattern of primitive and brutal life which we see in the animals' world — the survival of the fittest in the jungle. As long as we, human beings are divided by nations, states, and regions with separate and different norms and seeking their own selfish interests endorsed by the traditional naturalistic norms, we will never be able to create a cultural welfare society.

❖ Global Common Society

It is now time for us to transform our human society into a cultural-welfare society. In order to create this society, we must abandon the existing old world order such as exclusionistic nationalism constructed on the naturalistic norms, and must institute, at the initial stage, a new world order based on "regional cooperation societies" (RCS), ultimately to construct a "global common society" (GCS).

The good examples of RCS are the EC (now EU) in Europe, the OAS in Americas, the ASEAN in Southeast Asia, and the APEC in the Asia-Pacific area. At the first stage of reconstructing world order, viable regional organizations everywhere in close cooperation with the United Nations will invigorate regionally economic, cultural, and security cooperation which will strengthen regional peace and prosperity.

In order to consolidate further politically and administratively what the RCSs have functionally achieved, it is necessary for the RCSs to evolve into "regional integration society" (RIS) like the European Union which is in reality a confederation of the European states evolved from the European Community (EC).

The reality of today is that we are all living in single global society which requires us to have common goals, to think and act according to common norms, and to work together for common tasks. Sharing common goals, norms, and tasks, we must start to construct a new human society which is called "Oughtopia."

It is a desirable and realizable society as it ought to be and ought to do for mankind. It will be ideally a common human society which will be a spiritually beautiful, materially affluent, and humanly rewarding society for all mankind and which will bring about a true and permanent world peace.

History and our own contemporary experience teach us that we cannot achieve world peace with peace-loving and peace-keeping minds alone. In order to achieve a permanent world peace, we must reform first the global society towards the direction of internationalization, democratization, humanization and welfarization. We also know that structural peace devices such as the balance of power, collective security, and a unipolar system like Pax Romana have all failed to prevent war and to maintain peace since there are so many variable factors that trigger war.

Yet we are still clinging to exclusionary nationalism, the doctrine of class struggle and religious intolerance which are detrimental to the achieving of a permanent global peace and a true global civil society. We must remove these remnants of the past as we are now all the members of a single global community, breathing in one sphere of simultaneous life, being organized into a very close knitting interdependent relationship, and sharing a common destiny.

Therefore, only when we are able to achieve the five imperative conditions as mentioned above namely, (*a*) cultivation of the global democratic spirit, (*b*) reconstruction of human society, (*c*) universal democratic society, (*d*) proper social norms, and (*e*) global common society, we mankind can have a peaceful, co-operative, and co-prosperous global society that will set us free from an urge to or the necessity of war and aggression.

The broad objectives of Non-Violent Education [NVE] include—

- Promote non-violence values and attitudes (autonomy, responsibility, co-operation, creativity and solidarity);
- Learn to live together, respecting the differences and similarities;
- Develop a co-operative learning based on dialogue and intercultural understanding;
- To adopt non-violence solutions to conflicts through mediations and conflict-resolving strategies;
- Targeting the children and young people, particularly in the school educational process to integrate peace and non-violence in theory and practice; and

- Integrating non-violence in every aspect of teaching and learning processes, including curriculum development activities, teacher training and management of the educational institutions.

The United Nations General Assembly declared 2000 the International Year for a Culture of Peace and the Decade 2001-2010 as the International Decade for the Promotion of Non-Violence and Peace for the Children of the World.

❖ Strategies and Activities

SANKALP has been professing peace and non-violence as holistic concepts and practices that reject aggression and violence to achieve a peaceful society. The emphasis is on peaceful and constructive co-existence, and resolution of conflict and conflict-ridden situations. The historic contributions of two best known proponents of the theory and practice of non-violence, Mahatma Gandhi and Martin Luther King, which provide powerful strategies and advantages of non-violence, are sought to be propagated and disseminated by the Organisation.

The Organisation's activities on peace and human rights education are focused on a set of integrated activities, which include:

- Establishing and facilitating networks of Organisations, both non governmental and governmental to promote exchange of information, experiences and good practices on education for a culture of peace and non-violence;
- Involving the educational· institutions; with partnerships of the parents, local self--government and grassroots Organisations to promote human rights education;
- Orientation courses for the students;
- Capacity-building and training for teachers, teacher-educators and educational administrations;
- Integrating principles and strategies of non-violence and culture of peace into all subject areas and disciplines in the curriculum by taking into account the local realities and traditions, within the cultural diversity and international framework; and
- Promotion of advocacy of the principles and practices of non-violence and culture of peace in education by particularly involving the decision-makers and leaders of opinion.

Over the years the United Nations, particularly the UNESCO, have developed a number of standard-setting instruments, declarations and action plans; which are widely accepted by the international communities and which provided basic framework for promoting the concept of education for a culture of peace worldwide.

❖ Respect for Human Dignity

"What man has done to man has no limit. He has tortured him, he has burned him, he has killed him, he has exploited him in every possible way — religious, political, economic. This has seen the story of man to man; the clever exploit the stupid, the ignorant."

— J. Krishnamurti

The tradition of human rights concepts is as old as human civilization. Every society had varying norms to protect human life and dignity. Great religions strengthened the traditions.

Human rights can be broadly defined as those rights which human beings are entitled to which no one can deprive them of. They are a set of guarantees that ensure not only living but also those basic conditions to live with dignity as a human being. They are designed to protect individuals from the threat to life and human dignity.

❖ The Declaration of the Universal Human Rights by the United Nations

Organization is a moral victory of mankind as a whole in recent times. It is the culmination of the moral values that all religions advocated from the beginning of history. Now for the first time in history, the whole world has accepted a set of rights applied to every human being, irrespective of nationality, religion, sex, social status, occupation, wealth, property, or any other differentiating ethnic, cultural, or social characteristic. The declaration begins with the article: *"All human beings are born free and equal in dignity and rights. They are endowed with reason and conscience and should act towards one another in a spirit of brotherhood."*

The purpose of the declaration is obviously to provide a global foundation to protect human dignity. It subsequently initiated various States to adopt and enlarge the principles of human rights in the Constitutions. Many codes of rights, like African Charter on Human and People's Rights, European Convention on Human Rights and American Declaration of Rights and Duties of Man sprang up following it.

The declaration also led to include principles of human rights into various sections of public laws, such as race equality, sex discrimination, and court procedures. The declaration covers right to life, liberty, and security of person. Slavery, torture, cruel punishment, arbitrary arrest and detention, and invasion of privacy and family are banned. Due process of law is guaranteed using such principles as "innocent until proved guilty." Freedom of thought and speech, conscience and religious belief are accepted. Private ownership of property, freedom of movement, right to employment, health and education are also guaranteed. The Declaration covers such major areas like survival, dignity, political action, culture, and economic and social rights. However, the convention in the present form may not be perfect according to certain cultural perspectives because of the strong Western cultural influence in their make. At least, it has got to be accepted as a set of minimum moral standards required by all cultures.

Developing consciousness of rights is important in that they are strong factors in peace. Most of the conflicts arise from violation of human rights. Mere acceptance of the rights nationally or internationally alone is not sufficient. The political, cultural and economic diversities of the globe are so complex and therefore there is a need to have determined action to make human rights a reality in the societies. It is the responsibility of every citizen, government and civil organization to secure them.

From the child's early years, education for human rights is both practical and necessary. The secondary stage is more advanced than the elementary stage. Knowledge should now be presented more systematically so that their social behaviour should be developed in a nice way.

Every educational institution must lay the foundation for human rights. Human rights education aims at creating an attitude of respect for other people. Knowledge about human rights should lead on to activities that promote the law and the rights. The teacher should be the role model in upholding and spreading human rights. The child's knowledge and beliefs should find expression in discussion, posters and drawings, written texts including stories, games and songs. It is important for the teacher to develop in the learner through a multi pronged approach a sensitivity towards the rights of human beings.

Education should be child-centred and activity-based. As such learning the right of human beings cannot be a passive process in which the pupil is forced to follow on authoritarian teaching model. Social studies classes, especially civic, should focus on human rights democracy and peace since these are the foundations of citizenship. In addition to civics, all the subjects taught in school can contribute to the establishment of the concepts required for an understanding of human rights.

Children acquire through mass media knowledge about the on-going wars, the possibility of nuclear war and ecological catastrophies. The basic questions arising in the mind of a right thinking educationist would be:

1. How should schools deal with peace and war?
2. How can schools be instrumental in raising the possibilities for peaceful co-existence in future?
3. How can we provide some form of education for peace?
4. How can be prepare our young minds to live in peace with fellow human beings?
5. How can our future citizens of the globe be prepared to assume responsibilities?
6. How can be train, develop and foster peace through education?

Concludingly, it may be stated that our society is rapidly degrading. There is witnessed a rapid change because of new innovations. Each individual is getting involved in a cut-throat competition, and material achievement has really transformed the human being. Yet people remain frustrated and unhappy! Why? Because, people are really hungry and hunting for mental peace!

Peace is not merely the absence of active violence; it is something more positive. God has given us a life, the most precious thing in the world. But what have we done? We have distorted into pieces, divided it, brought about violence, destruction, hatred, lived a life without love, without compassion, without passion.

The greatest man is he who chooses the right with invincible resolution; who resists the temptation from within and without; who resists the temptation from within and without; who bears the heaviest burdens cheerfully; why is calmest in storms and most fearless under menace and frown; and whose reliance on truth, on virtue and on God, is most unfaltering.

Hatred is the vice of narrow souls; they feed it with all their littleness and make it the pretcxt of base tyrannies. Hence, a good teacher must keep himself or herself away from all this. The perfection of the teacher should not be reduce to a trade. It is a calling, a vocation, a mission. It is the duty of the teachers to make pupils good citizens of the new democracy. They must impart to the pupils zest for new experience, love for adventure in knowledge. Honesty of thought and speech must become ornaments of the teacher. Those who speak the truth are the only builders of a better life. Accordingly, a good teacher should be able to inculcate the concept of peace in his or her pupils. The teachers must be taught to instruct their pupils with examples and precepts. Present day curriculum of schools is mainly centred to material benefits Hence, teachers have to make use of some sort of strategy while teaching to their pupils.

Human rights education at all levels of education is most relevant. The students should know that education is an important human right in their daily lives. Education being concerned with human being and with their orientation for the future does play a fundamental role. It provides individuals with the capacity and motivation to act.

Hence, the teachers should try to teach about Human Rights to their children.

Let us try to know more about human rights in details.

HUMAN RIGHTS

1. Introduction

Ancient Indian literature and Indian philosophy, and Indian Constitution show the existence of Human rights. Indian democracy is one of the biggest democracy in world directly show the equity, liberty brotherhood in its permeable. The elements of Human rights are generated from gross roots of Indian philosophy. In ancient India, all communities have their laws and rules which reflect the today morals and values of Human rights. Some of them are considered as Universal rights. Slogan from Marathi "Vishvachi Maze Ghar" (Universe is my home) which contains the spirits of Human rights. The Rig Veda, Atharva Veda and specially Buddhist philosophy advocates the equity, freedom and brotherhood. In context of pre-independence era, Indian people, freedom fighters were struggled with British government for their rights. The pre-independence leader, Lokmanya Bal Gangadhar Tilak asserted that, "Swaraj is my births right and I will have it." All these pre-independence ethos and Indian Buddhist philosophy provides a sound moral foundations for human rights.

"I learned from my illiterate but wise mother that all rights to be deserved and preserved came from duty well done. Thus the very right to live accrues to us when we do the duty of citizenship of the world. From this, one fundamental statement, perhaps it is easy enough to define duties of man and woman and cor-relate every right to some corresponding duty to be first performed ...."

— **Mahatma Gandhi**

The recent NCF 2009 for Teacher Educators as proposed by NCERT (National Council of Educational Research and Training), India focuses on: Perspectives for Equitable and Sustainable Development. In order to develop future citizens who promote equitable and sustainable development for all sections of society and respect for all, it is necessary that they be educated through perspectives of gender equity, the perspectives that develop values for peace, respect the rights of all, and respect and value work. In the present ecological crisis, promoted by extremely commercialized and competitive life-styles, teachers and children need to be educated to change their consumption patterns and the way they look at natural resources (NCF 2009. P 13.)

2. Concepts and meaning of Human Rights

It can be defined as the basic standards without which humankind cannot live in dignity as human beings. Human rights are the foundation of freedom, justice and peace.

Human rights are rights to all human beings, whatever our nationality origin, colour, religion, language, race, sex and any other status. We are equally entitled to our human rights without discrimination. These rights are all interrelated, interdependent, and indivisible.

3. What is Human Rights Education

Human rights education is a education about the rights of human beings: rights of inherent, rights are indivisible, rights are inalienable, and rights are universal.

4. Human Rights Education Competencies

(*a*) **Communication with target group:** Teacher should familiar with these skills while communicating with group or individual one particularly in classroom.

(*b*) **Knowledge, information and data collection:** Before communicating with the group teacher should collect all information and knowledge in accordance with human rights education

(*c*) **International brotherhood for peace and harmony** teacher should well acquaint with cultivation, promotion and protection of International understanding and brotherhood for peace and harmony.

(*d*) **Lovingness, passionate and respect:** The related values and morals should inculcate.

(*e*) **Leading leadership initiative to control violations:** Related skills and attitudes should be developed.

(*f*) **National and International understanding:** Related skills and attitudes should be incorporated among the teacher.

5. Characteristics of Human Rights

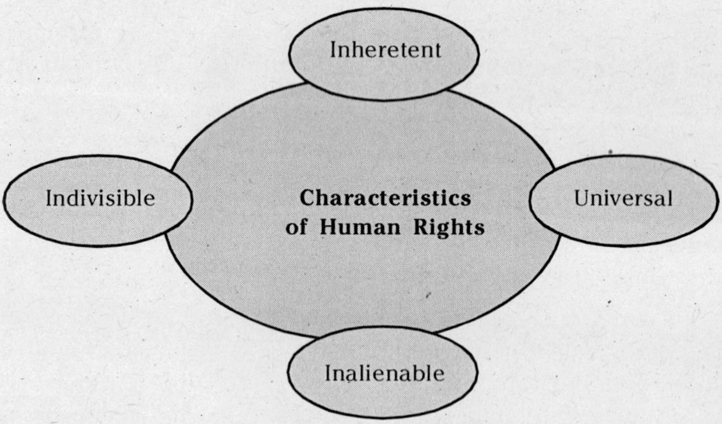

(a) Inherent

Human rights do not have to be bought, earned or inherited; they belong to people simply because they are human. So human rights are inherent to each individual.

(b) Human rights are Universal

These are same for all human beings regardless of race, sex, and religion, political, national or social origin. We are all born free, equal in dignity and rights so human rights are universal.

(c) Human rights are Inalienable

Human rights cannot be taken away no one has right to deprive another person of them for any reason.

(d) Human rights are indivisible

All human rights are indivisible whether those rights may be right to life, equality before the law and freedom expression, economic, social and cultural rights.

6. Need of Human Rights Education

Human Rights education of humankind is begins from their family so it is necessary to have human rights education from their parents and society. If we make a survey of our society about human rights education very few groups or individuals might be aware about the term human rights. Thought they know the term human rights but they did not know what exact or proper meaning of human rights is in 10th December 1948 the UNC declaration of human rights and made on International Human Rights day. Though the resolution bills passed by UNO and they prepared some watch committees they are number of events are occurring against of these rights. In this contest it is our duty to transfer, to inculcate, to make aware to focus the light and spread the knowledge of H.R in society for betterment of our future generation and generate the peace and harmony and related values among every one.

1. In accordance with 21st generation future which should be free from all kinds of tensions. There is an urgent need to inculcate Human right in everyone.
2. To promote peaceful and happiness climate among the society.
3. To avoid the violence events, issues/liberty, equality, justice.
4. Human rights are the prerequisites for promoting/fostering the peace in society.

(7) Promotion and Protection of Human Rights Education

Teacher Educator should be:

1. Motivate the students to establish Human rights club in college. The members of club watch the events against of human rights.

2. Organizing human rights related street plays, dramas so the awareness may be lightening up among the citizens.
3. Invite the students to express their views.
4. Invite the students to sort out make the collection of Issues related to human rights from Newspaper and other sources.
5. Organizing debate competitions, elocution speech In accordance with human rights.
6. Foster to celebration of 10th December, Human Rights day by organizing various programs such as essay competitions, speech competitions and so forth.
7. Motivates the learner by arranging or organize the workshops, seminar, and by providing human right information tool kit.
8. Motivate the learner to ask questioning in accordance with HRE session and students exchange their views, ideas in these session.
9. Able to foster and reflect the human rights through their body language and attitudinal expressions.
10. Motivate to prepare a project work on human rights by which awareness may be aroused.

❖ Recommendation

1. Human rights education should be a part of every ones education .which may foster the development of human values and duties.
2. The curriculum should be reformed in advent of the human rights education.
3. Teachers should be well prepared to develop and inculcation human rights perspectives and skills among their students.
4. Teachers should be prepared in context of international understanding.
5. Seminars, workshops, symposium should be conducted through NCERT and SCERT for in-service teacher education.
6. The curriculum should be reformed in advent of pre-service teacher education.

7. The teacher educations may develop a learning package that will help to transform the learners in developing critical attitudes into active participation, conviction that human rights must be protected, respected and promoted.
8. Students should be prepared in accordance with international understanding, peace, cooperation and education relating to human right and fundamental freedom.
9. Teacher educators should be able to acquire and update interdisciplinary knowledge, world problems and problems concerning with international cooperation.
10. Teacher educators must be actively participated in devising international education programme.
11. The role of teacher educator should be changed accordingly from knowledge transmitter to facilitator, implementer, community partner, action researcher and curriculum developer.
12. Teacher educators should be encouraging students to celebrate the human rights day and related activities.
13. Teacher educators should be encouraging students to organize symposium, seminars, conferences related to human rights education.
14. Teacher educators should be encouraging students to establish the Human rights violations watch clubs in school and society.
15. Teacher educators should be encouraging students to discuss or to express their views, ideas in promotion and protection of human rights education.
16. Teacher educators should encourage students to adopt participative, interactive, storytelling and so forth teaching methodologies in their teaching.
17. Teacher educators should encourage students to collect and identify the incidents, pictures, magazines etc. in relating human rights violations.

❖ Conclusion

Human rights education is an important aspect to bring the peace and harmony in society. Human rights education should be included at all levels and reframed time to time because inculcation of deep respect for human rights and fundamental freedoms are the supreme goals of education. Without equity, liberty and justice, dignity, it is impossible to promote and cultivate the peace, tolerance, and harmony in the society.

❖ Education of Human Rights

Schools have the responsibility to educate the next generation on human rights and inculcate the basic values imbedded in there. Although many curricula have it as a unit generally it is taught only at the cognitive level. Such academic learning has little impact on the actual behaviour. Merely memorizing the articles in the convention does not go far. What is necessary is to help learning them in a manner that the respect for human dignity is internalized and be a part of one's character. We have yet to search for effective methods of teaching human rights.

One of the critiques of the present approach to teaching rights is that it ignores the responsibility side. In the West, we see the overstress for the rights has led to imbalance of civic consciousness and human relationships. Campaigns that propagate human rights rarely speak about duties that go with them. Therefore, the message that people get is "Fight for your rights; neglect your duties." In the Orient, the emphasis is always given to one's duties before rights. There is an interesting Buddhist discourse called Sigalowada Sutta, which reflects the Oriental attitude to rights. Therein the Buddha explains that parents are bound to do their rightful to children when children perform their duties to parents. Masters are bound to do their rightful to workers when they perform their duties to masters. One has to earn one's rights by performing the duties. They are inseparable as the two sides of the same coin.

Concludingly, it may be said, then that peace is not just the absence of violence. It is basically a process constructed through research, training and practice. It focuses mainly on the response to a changing environment. Peace is a positive sign in history bringing people together, eliminating suspicion and mistrust. Put into simpler language, when one wants to talk on peace, he or she expects at least three basic conditions: Communication, Cooperation and Confidence. The ideal is to have the three of them working at the same time. UNESCO's constitution highlights these as pre-requisite in the preamble "ignorance of each others ways and lives has been a common cause, throughout the history of mankind, of that suspicion and mistrust between the peoples of the world through which their differences have all too often broken into war."

Ignorance is the main result of lack of communication: Suspicion and mistrust show that confidence building has not taken place; the fact that differences take into armed conflicts indicates that cooperative techniques have failed to give tangible results. We still have to make ourselves clear to answer such questions as —

— What is peace-education?

— What is the language of peace-education?

— How different cultures interpret peace-education?

— What new philosophical basis is required for the future of peace-education?

The future of peace-education as a philosophy needs fresh re-thinking in particular in relation into the following areas of study:

- The evaluation of peace-education and its place in education programmes and societies.
- The theoretical and pedagogical approaches to peace-education.
- Peace-education and value-based perspective.
- Research and curriculum development.
- Concept of peace-education in various cultures.
- Peace-education in science and technology.
- Peace-education and formal system of education.

Let us now peep through are more agency entitled 'IAEWP.'

International Association of Educators for World Peace (IAEWP) was affiliated with five specialized agencies of United Nations, Viz. UNESCOSIC, UNDPI, UNICEF, UNCED, UNESCO. They are promoting University education throughout the world through more than 100 chapters by encouraging development of Colleges and Universities for peace research. Support of UN-efforts in this regard, and of developing the kind of education, will contribute to the formation of characters capable of delaying aggression. So that conflict situations may be solved in positive manner.

In 1998, IAEWP was sponsored for the establishment of the Global Open University for world peace in Italy. The purpose of making university education is to reach all to be enlightened, for being helpful in building a non-exploitative, nonviolent and peaceful democratic society.

❖ Some Genuine Proposal for Peace University Education

1. Pursue the truth might turn pacifists in all free universities, re-planned to build peace.
2. University education should be free for all rich and poor. Merit should be criteria, not money.
3. Seek funds from donors like rich persons, industrialists, philanthropists, alumni-alumnae.
4. Abolish armies and destroy arms and ammunition; divert this money for peace University Education.
5. Impartial selection of meritorious teachers and non-teaching staff in the university.
6. Better service conditions are to be provided to teachers and non-teaching staff.
7. A National Directory of unemployed highly qualified persons holding Ph.D. or D.Litt. or D.Sc. in different disciplines. A reasonable pay and appointments are given.
8. Professional education must be de-linked from the university. For example medical, engineering and agriculture education must be attached with hospitals, industries and farms respectively.
9. The Peace University must be autonomous with national character.
10. The university should train men and women to think themselves and ultimately to the whole world.
11. In universities, at least, feeling of love and brotherhood among all communities should be fostered.
12. The students of a university should be trained to struggle against ignorance, injustice, oppression and fear of all men of whole world, and for international understanding and peace.
13. The University should create attitude favourable to the values necessary for a peaceful progressive and democratic governments in different parts of world.
14. The University must render support to the United Nations.
15. The University must teach peace, disarmament, human rights and about NGOs, United Nations, UNESCO, and other agencies of UN.

16. The university should be a sanctuary of international awakening and peace, and a lighthouse of perpetual learning.
17. The University should produce save leaders for mankind.
18. The Universities must be looked after by a Ministry of Peace in the Nation for smooth running of national universities to serve the cause of Peace.
19. There must be a University for Peace in each nation having affiliation with the United Nations.
20. Last but not the least, the university must develop a global common society — a society which would be spiritually beautiful, materially affluent and humanly rewarding.

Thus the role of a university should be to preserve, to develop and to create a culture of peace and ultimately its mission should be to build peace for the new millennium.

❖ UN's Peace Building Commission

Kofi Annan, Secretary General UNO at World Summit 2005 proposed to establish a new body of peace commission. A round 50% of the conflict of the past 20 years have recurred within five years of peace agreements. The commission will act only by consensus, proposing integrated strategies for stabilizing economic recovery and development and improving co-ordination. 31 members committee was formed to make a detail action programme (UN News, 2006).

The Greek philosopher's ideas, principles, theories, laws, formulas, preaching and practices, for which they were humiliated, tortured, and killed are the real foundations of University curriculum. Their statements are the true spirit of university.

Kyung Hee University, Seoul Republic of Korea (1949-99) is also the real symbol of true university spirit. Because its main function is to restore humanity and mortality for the creation of a global society on the principles of United Nations. Its purpose is "The creation of a civilized world." Its philosophy is democratization of school, ideas and living. Since 1949, this international peace university has been educating the young men to create a better living for mankind. The Global University was found by great world peace educator professor (Dr.) Young Seek Choue, who was himself a living symbol of university spirit. Kyung Hee University has been extending its knowledge beyond the campus through "the creation of new civilized work" serving national and global society through sharing its knowledge with 161 universities of the world. These universities should share the common mission of building peace for the new millennium.

In 1945, the United Nations was established to "save succeeding generations from the scourge of war," "to reaffirm faith in the... dignity and worth of the human person [and] in the equal rights of men and women", "to establish conditions under which justice and respect for the obligations arising from treaties and other sources of international law can be maintained," and "to promote social progress and better standards of life in larger freedom ...". (Preamble to the UN Charter □→)

Peace-education thus has developed as a means to achieve these goals. It is education that is "directed to the full development of the human personality and to the strengthening of respect for human rights and fundamental freedoms." It promotes "understanding, tolerance and friendship among all nations, racial or religious groups" and furthers "the activities of the United Nations for the maintenance of peace." (Article 26, Universal Declaration of Human Rights □→)

In other words, peace-education is an integral part of the work of the United Nations. Through a humanising process of teaching and learning, peace-educators facilitate human development. They strive to counteract the dehumanisation of poverty, prejudice, discrimination, rape, violence, and war.

UNICEF and UNESCO are particularly active advocates of education for peace. UNICEF describes peace-education as schooling and other educational initiatives that:

- Function as 'zones of peace', where children are safe from violent conflict.
- Uphold children's basic rights.
- Develop a climate that models peaceful and respectful behaviour among all members of the learning community.
- Demonstrate the principles of equality and non-discrimination in administrative policies and practices.
- Draw on the knowledge of peace-building that exists in the community, including means of dealing with conflict that are effective, non-violent, and rooted in the local culture.
- Handle conflicts in ways that respect the rights and dignity of all involved.

- Integrate an understanding of peace, human rights, social justice and global issues throughout the curriculum whenever possible.
- Provide a forum for the explicit discussion of values of peace and social justice.
- Use teaching and learning methods that stress participation, Cupertino, problem-solving and respect for differences.
- Enable children to put peace-making into practice in the educational setting as well as in the wider community.
- Generate opportunities for continuous reflection and professional development of all educators in relation to issues of peace, justice and rights. *(Peace-education in UNICEF Working Paper Series, July 1999).*

Many teachers are already practising peace-education without calling it by name. Historically, in various parts of the world, peace-education has been referred to as Education for Conflict Resolution, International Understanding, and Human Rights; Global Education; Critical Pedagogy; Education for Liberation and Empowerment; Social Justice Education Environmental Education; Life Skills Education; Disarmament and Development Education; and more. These various labels Illuminate the depth and diversity of the field. Using the term peace-education helps co-ordinate such global initiatives and unite educators in the common practice of educating for culture of peace.

Peace-education is about empowering people with the skills, attitudes, and knowledge:

- to build, maintain, and restore relationships at all levels of human interaction.
- to develop positive approaches towards dealing with conflicts — from the personal to the international.
- to create safe environments, both physically and emotionally, that nurture each individual.
- to create a safe world based on justice and human rights.
- to build a sustainable environment and protect it from exploitation and war.

World peace organizations are finally starting to get more attention. In the wake of many turbulent situations around the world, it seems that some people are finally starting to see the light. This is directly due to the unending work of several world peace organizations. We would like to take a moment to truly appreciate and think about all of the wonderful things that these peace organizations have done for us. This is all in hopes that they will continue to spread peace and that one day, we will live together in tolerance and peace.

Here are some world peace organizations that we would consider to be especially dedicated to the cause:

- American Friends Service Committee
- Amnesty International
- Nonviolent Peaceforce
- Pax Christi
- Peace Coup
- Peaceworkers UK
- Seeds of Peace
- Spirit of the Sword
- World Peace Council
- Ulster Project International
- Peacekeeping

Since these world peace organizations have done so much work to support humanity, it is time for humanity to start supporting them.

The first 20th century peace movements were born between the two wars, that is in the twenties and thirties, and gave rise to the League of Nations. Unfortunately, the League failed in its quest because the member States had not succeeded in endowing the League with the instruments needed to establish peace, such as our modern-day peacekeepers. The rise in the nationalist movements of the 19th and 20th centuries that provoked the two world wars played, according to some, a major role in the idea of creating the conditions for world peace. World War I took the lives of more than 9 million people, killing between 20% to 25% of the male population of France and Germany. As for World War II, 55 million people died, including 6 million Jews in the Nazi concentration camps.

Faced with the largest catastrophes in human history, men and women around the planet began to dream of a better, peaceful world.

Thus, shortly after World War II, on October 24, 1945, 51 States ratified the United Nations Charter with the hope of freeing our world from the possibility of war. The UN was thus created and equipped with instruments that its predecessor lacked. The UN established several programs intended to reduce, as much as possible, all the factors leading to outbreaks in conflicts. These programs did not only focus on peace keepers, who intervene after a conflict has erupted, but also on economic and social development, human rights, and the struggle to end world poverty and hunger. Indeed, all of these United Nations programs contribute directly or indirectly to the prevention of conflicts and thus to peace on earth. It is certainly true that, in the last 50 years, not everyone in the world has known peace, but it is gradually gaining ground. The dream of peace in the World is becoming less and less utopian and more and more attainable.

The United Nations is an international organisation of countries. It was created for many reasons:

- There should be peace and security in the world after the Second World War.
- Countries should be friendly to each other.
- Countries should help each other solve problems.
- Human rights should be respected everywhere in the world.

After the Second World War, the allied countries got together to discuss in which ways such an organization could be created. In 1945, 50 countries got together in San Francisco and signed an agreement that created the United Nations. The United States invited the new UN to set up its headquarters in New York. The building was finished in 1952 and has been the permanent seat of the UN until today.

❖ Membership

Membership is open to all peace-loving nations. Today, there are about 200 countries in the UN — only very few have not become members.

Switzerland joined the UN in 2002 because the Swiss always wanted to be neutral.

❖ Peacekeepers

The United Nations Peacekeeping Forces are groups of soldiers who help keep peace in places of conflict. Most of the time they are observers or soldiers who don't have so many weapons. Normally, they try to keep the enemies away from each other.

The first UN peacekeepers were sent to the Middle East in 1948 after the first war between Israel and its neighbours. After many weeks of war, the UN peacekeepers were able to help make peace. Since then UN soldiers have helped patrol borders between Israel and Syria.

UN soldiers have also helped in Cyprus — a small island in the Mediterranean Sea that has mostly Greek people, but the northern part is settled by Turks. UN peacekeepers control a border that divides the north and the south of the island.

In the 1980s and 90s UN peacekeepers have helped keep peace in many countries. In the middle of the 1990s, they were sent to former Yugoslavia to keep peace between the Serbs, Croats and Muslims.

UN peacekeepers are sent to a region only if the Security Council tells them to. They can only help keep peace if all the other countries agree, and they may use their weapons only if they are attacked. Most of them wear a blue hat or a helmet so that you can tell if they are UN soldiers.

Since 1948 there have been 54 UN peacekeeping operations all over the world. Over 120 countries have sent Soldiers.

❖ Achievements

- The UN has helped many countries become democratic and peaceful states.
- The UN plays an important role in protecting our environment. The "Earth Summit" in Rio de Janeiro in 1992 was a big conference about climate control other problems of our environment.
- The International Atomic Energy Agency is a UN organisation that controls the nuclear weapons of countries and sees to it that they don't build an atomic bomb.
- Since 1950, the UN has given help to over 50 million refugees. These people had to leave their countries because of war, hunger or diseases.

- Africa is the poorest continent in our world. The UN has given African countries money and other kinds of help so that they can feed people and give them work to do.
- It helps give developing countries safe and clean water.
- It fights drug abuse and improves the lives of children who live in poverty.
- It helps people learn how to read and write.
- It helps farmers in poor countries where it is too hot or too dry.

♣♣♣

BIBLIOGRAPHY

Aranha, M. Education for Peace: Guidelines for Indian Schools, Mumbai, 1989.

Bey, T.M. and G.Y. Turner: Making School a Place of Peace, London, Sage Publications.

Barash, D.P.: Introduction to Peace Studies, California University of Washington.

Balsooriya, A.S. Management of Conflicts in Schools, Maharagama, Sri Lanka: National Institute of Education.

Bigge, D.: In Our Own Backyard: A Teachers' Guide For Rights of the Child: Toronto: UNICEF.

Balsooriya, A.S. : Teaching Peace to Children. Maharagama, Sri Lanka: National Institute of Education.

Cooper, P.: The Development of the Concept of War — Journal of Peace Research, Vol. 2, No. 1, pg. 1 to 17.

Cotrina Abrams, G. Educatioin For Peace. Miami Beach.

Dewey, J. Education & Democracy, New York Free Press.

Deolars, J. Learning the Treasure Within: Report of the International Commission for the 21st Century: Paris: UNESCO.

Dhand, H. (2000) Teaching Human Rights — A Handbook For Teacher Educators — Bhopal: Asian Institute of Human Rights Education.

Digmurti, R. — Global Perceptions on Peace Education — Discovery Publication House, New Delhi.

Galtung, J. and D. Ikeda — Choose Peace London: Pluto Press.

Galtung, J.: There Are Alternatives; Four Roads to Nottigrahm: Russel Press.

Galtung, J: Violence, Peace & Peace Research, Journal of Peace Research 6(3): 167-191.

Galtung, J.: Peace by Peaceful Means: London Sage Publications.

Harris, I.M.: Peace Education, Jefferson NC McFarland & Co.

Hicks, D.: Education for Peace, Ronteledge: London.

Herzog, S. Joy: In the Classroom, Boulder Greek, California: University of the Tree Press.

Hutchinson, F.P.: Education Beyond Violent Futures. London: Routledge.

Harris, I. and Mary Lee (2003) Peace Education, 2nd ed. Jefferson, N.C. McFarland.

Harris, I. (2004) Peace Education Theory, Journal of Peace Education 1(1): 5-20.

Isonhart, M.W. & Spangle, M. (2000): Collaborative Approaches to Resolving Conflict, pp. 23-28, 45, 55 and 71-85.

Maria, D. [2003]: "Value Education For Peace" The CTE Journal, 2(3): 25.

Maria, Roopa (2008): Peace Education, New Frontiers In Education: Vol. 41, No. 14.

Nieto, S. (1992): Affirming Diversity, White Plains: New York, London.

Pandey, S. (2004): Education for Peace: Self Instructional Package For Teacher Educators.

Read, Herbert. Education for Peace. New York: Harper, Colophon.

Reardo, B.A. Tolerance — The Threshold For Peace: UNESCO.

Saxena, N.R. and Chaturvedi Sikha (2003): Education in Emerging Indian Society, Meerut: R.L. Lall Book Depot.

Thousand Oaks (Ca) Sage Publications.

♣♣♣